EPIC ATHLETES
ZION WILLIAMSON

Dan Wetzel
Illustrations by David SanAngelo

Henry Holt and Company
New York

Henry Holt and Company, *Publishers since 1866*
Henry Holt® is a registered trademark of Macmillan Publishing Group, LLC
120 Broadway, New York, NY 10271 • mackids.com

Our books may be purchased in bulk for promotional, educational, or business use.
Please contact your local bookseller or the Macmillan Corporate
and Premium Sales Department at (800) 221-7945 ext. 5442 or
by email at MacmillanSpecialMarkets@macmillan.com.

Library of Congress Cataloging-in-Publication Data is available.

First edition, 2021 / Designed by Elynn Cohen

Printed in the United States of America
by LSC Communications, Harrisonburg, Virginia

ISBN 978-1-250-76233-7

1   3   5   7   9   10   8   6   4   2

The 4th quarter of Zion Williamson's NBA debut...

 SA 99 NO 91

"Zion stepping back..."

"... and hitting a three!"

 NO 94

1

Opening Night

Z<small>ION</small> W<small>ILLIAMSON</small> wasn't smiling. He wasn't laughing. He wasn't bouncing around the basketball court in joy. That was the most obvious sign that something wasn't right, that his long-awaited, injury-delayed NBA debut wasn't going as planned.

Zion doesn't just play the game of basketball, he plays it with the excitability of a puppy. Flying through the air. Hammering down dunks. Quick jumps and changes of direction. Long bounce passes through a pack of defenders. Zion brings happiness to people watching him play, all while being the picture of happiness himself.

He is a showman, an actor who is the star of the play, the recording artist feeding off the fans at his own concert.

"When you're able to get the ball and you're wide open and you see the crowd standing on their feet, to describe that feeling, you have to be in that situation," Zion said of his thought process before delivering a breathtaking dunk. "The ball is in your hands with thousands of people watching you, and they're just waiting to see what you're going to do."

Only this time, in his first game for the New Orleans Pelicans, a debut that had been delayed nearly three months due to minor surgery on his right knee, Zion looked tense. He looked nervous. He looked stiff. And those are three words that are never used to describe Zion Williamson on a basketball court.

In the rare moments back in college when Zion wasn't dominating the game, his coach, Duke's Mike Krzyzewski, would pull him aside and offer the simplest advice.

"Smile," Coach K would say. "Have fun."

Zion would usually exhale and go back to being

Zion—a six-foot-seven, 285-pound force of nature, grabbing rebounds, making steals, and, of course, soaring to the rim to deliver some kind of mighty dunk—maybe a windmill, maybe a 360. He'd go back to having a good time playing the game he loved.

That was how he'd started playing basketball, after all. First with his friends, then in rec leagues in Florence, South Carolina, where he was coached by his mother, a former college high jumper, and his stepdad, a former Division I basketball player. If it wasn't fun, why do it?

He liked to work hard and practice his fundamentals, but mostly he liked to play. No matter what was going on in his life, he could always step on a court and forget about his problems. That didn't change when he became a social media star and top recruit in high school, or when he was a household name—just "Zion"—during a year at Duke University. And it shouldn't now as he entered the NBA as the most hyped rookie since LeBron James in 2003.

"I know everybody uses this corny little caption on social media, but it's true for me," Zion said. "The moment I stop having fun playing basketball is the moment I'll be done."

Zion wasn't about to stop playing, not when his NBA career was, literally, just beginning. But he needed a spark to get back to being . . . well, Zion.

Over eighteen thousand fans had come to watch Zion and the Pelicans play the San Antonio Spurs. Some hometown fans had paid nearly $1,000 for a single ticket to get their first glimpse of the man they dreamed would bring them championships one day. All over New Orleans there had been a buzz of anticipation for what was to come, with fans jamming into bars and restaurants or their friends' living rooms to watch. A huge national television audience tuned in to see what the kid could do against NBA competition. ESPN had been hyping the game for days.

The plan was to bring Zion along slowly. Team doctors wanted him playing about four minutes at the start of each quarter. Then they wanted him to rest while they examined his knee. It wasn't an ideal way to start a career, but it was the only way Zion could play at all, so he agreed to the plan. The doctors and coaches were thinking about his long-term future.

"I think you have to be smart about it," said New Orleans coach Alvin Gentry.

With those limitations in place, the game wasn't going as well as Zion had hoped. He'd played about twelve minutes through the first three quarters, but scored just five points. He'd taken only three shots. He'd committed four turnovers. He wasn't in the flow of the action, where he would naturally find the ball and overwhelm opponents.

The Pelican fans, who'd come seeking a vision of greatness, were getting restless. So were the people watching on TV. On social media, where critics love to overreact, some were wondering if Zion's knee injury meant he would never be as good as he had been in college and high school. Others thought he might have been overrated. This was the NBA, not college ball.

Or maybe this was proof that a player with Zion's huge, muscular build couldn't last in the NBA without injuries impacting his game.

Zion wasn't scrolling through Twitter and Instagram during the game, but the look on his face suggested that he knew he was disappointing a lot of people.

"You don't have to make the Hall of Fame tonight," teammate J.J. Redick told him. "Just go out and be you. The rest will sort of take care of itself."

Zion walked onto the court in the fourth quarter and it looked like more of the same. He was hesitant. He looked uncomfortable. He wasn't aggressive. He missed a six-foot shot. He committed another turnover.

Then with 8:52 remaining in the game, Zion got the ball and found himself unguarded out behind the three-point line. He wasn't known as a three-point shooter, although he'd worked tirelessly to improve his form, especially when he was out of action because of his knee. Putting up shots was the one thing doctors had allowed Zion to do during the rehab process because it wouldn't impact the injury.

He also knew he'd be coming out of the game soon, likely at the eight-minute mark. Might as well let one fly, right?

He did. It went in.

The fans erupted in cheers, but as Zion got back to play defense, there was still no smile. Next time down the court on offense, Zion went down low near the basket and broke free from a Spur defender. Teammate Lonzo Ball saw what was happening and lobbed a pass near the hoop. Zion rose up, caught it over two San Antonio defenders, and laid it in.

Now the crowd was going wild! This was the Zion they had expected.

Still, no smile.

Next time down, he nailed another wide-open three. Then he secured a defensive rebound. Back on offense, he received a pass down on the post near the basket, made a startlingly quick move, and laid the ball up. It missed, but with the otherworldly speed of his reaction, Zion seized the rebound and scored.

No smile, but he was bouncing back down the court now. He was beginning to look like himself again. This here—now, this was basketball.

The game clock was ticking fast, though, and Zion was supposed to come out of the game, per doctor's orders. He was on a roll, however, and as long as there wasn't a stoppage in play, there was nothing Coach Gentry could do.

Next possession—a Zion three-pointer. Possession after that—another Zion three-pointer. He was on fire, so what could his teammates do but continue to feed him the rock?

Finally, he got it again and was fouled. He hit one of two free throws and then, seconds later, was taken out of the game because team doctors were shouting at Coach Gentry.

"He wasn't happy about it," Coach Gentry said. "I don't think anyone would be happy about it. I ain't the brightest coach in the world, but I wasn't going to take him out in those situations unless I was told to."

San Antonio would go on to win the game. Coach Gentry had to ignore the crowd chanting "We want Zion!" in the final minutes. Still, Zion's first game was a success.

In a three-minute, eight-second stretch, Zion had scored 17 points. He finished with 22 total and put the NBA on notice: Yes, he was the real deal.

"It was everything I dreamed of except for the losing," Zion said. "Just the energy the crowd brought, the energy the city brought, it was electric. I'm just grateful."

And as he left the court to a standing ovation, he slapped hands with teammates and even briefly broke into a smile.

The game, for Zion Williamson, was fun again, and when Zion is having fun out on the court, there might not be anyone anywhere who is capable of stopping him.

SA 101   NO 94

"Here's a lob to Zion..."

2

Secret Weapons

ZION LATEEF WILLIAMSON was born July 6, 2000, in Salisbury, North Carolina. He was named after Mount Zion—the legendary hill in Israel, right outside the Old City of Jerusalem. "It's a biblical name," Zion would explain.

He had to spend time explaining to people how to pronounce his name. It's "ZEYE-on" not "ZEE-on." For too long, people were confused. Little did they know he would make the name famous across the sports world.

This was long before he became an NBA star;

before he was making crowds *ooh* and *ahh* at shots he blocked while playing for Duke University; before he was a six-foot-seven sixteen-year-old who was dunking in high school games. Growing up, he was just another happy kid living in South Carolina, where his mother had moved them.

Zion is in the pros now, but he didn't dream that big when he was little. His ultimate goal was to be a college basketball star. Maybe that was because not a lot of people expected him to grow so tall and get so strong. Maybe not even Zion himself.

But Zion had a secret weapon: his mom.

Her name is Sharonda Sampson and she was a track athlete in the 1970s at Livingstone College. It's a small school in North Carolina that was actually once called the Zion Wesley Institute. The Livingstone campus is where the first Black intercollegiate football game was played in America, back in 1892. Sharonda attended school there nearly one hundred years later. She was a tremendous talent, routinely clearing six feet in the high jump—leaping ability she obviously had passed on to her son.

It was Sharonda who put five-year-old Zion on a basketball team with nine-year-old kids, always encouraging him to pass the ball to them. That was smart for two reasons: It helped Zion get along with the older boys, and it helped him learn the skills of a point guard. Back then, no one knew Zion would grow up to be so tall. At his size, Sharonda thought that if he was going to fulfill his dream of being a college basketball player, he'd better learn how to pass. And so he did.

Sharonda also told her son that he would need to work very hard and stay out of trouble if he was going to chase his basketball dream. It wasn't enough just to play; he would have to practice as much as or more than any other kid out there. He would have to wake up early to practice, and sometimes stay up late to practice. And if basketball earned him a lot of attention, he would have to stay focused on school and his game—not fame.

Zion gets his middle name, Lateef, from his biological father, Lateef Williamson. He too was a great athlete in his prime. Lateef was a six-foot-five, 260-pound defensive lineman who was so good at high school football that a lot of colleges wanted him to play on their teams. At first Lateef went to North Carolina State in Raleigh, but then he transferred to Livingstone, where he met Sharonda.

Zion is their only child, a son with the strength

and power of his father and the grace and leaping ability of his mother. "God-given athleticism" is how Zion often described it.

But he also had another secret weapon: his stepdad.

Lee Anderson knew hoops, too. He had lived Zion's dream of playing college basketball back in the 1970s at Clemson University in South Carolina. You may know Clemson for its championship football program, but they play some good basketball too, and Zion's stepdad was a part of it. He wasn't a star player by any means—he scored just sixteen points in his college career—but you can't even get to that level of basketball without being a great high school talent. Mostly, he understood how the game should be played and the amount of hard work it took to make it to the top.

Lee's playing career was derailed when he was hit by a car. He said he prayed about his future and believed he would have another chance at a basketball life. It turned out that he would: Lee would become a coach for kids, and he would help Sharonda coach Zion.

After college, Sharonda had moved to Florence, South Carolina, about 150 miles south of Livingstone. She'd gotten a job there as a schoolteacher after she broke up with Lateef, and that's where she met Lee. They chose to raise their family there, and years later, they'd have a son of their own, Noah.

Zion didn't play just basketball growing up, he played almost every sport, including football and soccer. When Zion played for the youth basketball association in Florence, he was allowed to play for only twenty-four minutes a game, just like every other kid. But Zion wanted to stay in the *whole* game because he was very competitive and he loved basketball so much.

But just because he loved the game of basketball didn't mean that he immediately found *his* game on the court as a kid.

"I sucked," Zion said in an interview with *SLAM* magazine. "But playing the game of basketball, it's like a love—my first love."

As much as he wanted to win, he always kept in mind what his mom had taught him about passing the ball and helping his friends. And with time, he improved. When he was in the fifth grade, Zion's team won a local tournament and he was named the MVP. But at the awards ceremony, he did something shocking: He gave the trophy to a teammate who had scored hardly any points during the entire tournament.

Why did Zion do this? He explained that his teammate had scored his first basket during the tournament, and that that meant a lot to his friend and to everyone else. So Zion unselfishly gave his friend the trophy.

Even at a young age, some of the people who watched Zion play sensed that he was special. "Sometimes it doesn't dawn on you as parents," Sharonda told *The Charlotte Observer*. "But all the time, when he was growing up playing, he stood out among his peers. When you have elderly people come to watch and they don't know who you are, and they're saying this boy will be special and we'll see him on TV, you start to think there may be something to this."

There were other factors that also made Zion a rare talent. He is left-handed, which is uncommon in a lot of sports. It served him well in basketball. Defenders would guard his right side, expecting him to shoot with that hand. Then he'd put the ball in his left and flip it up easily.

Zion went to Johnakin Middle School in Marion, South Carolina, about twenty-two miles away from Florence. His mother taught physical education and coached the basketball team at Johnakin. Zion was about five-nine and 120 pounds then, and he was a good player. He scored about 20 points a game, and helped Johnakin win a local championship.

That wasn't enough for his mother, though. She wasn't some easygoing coach who favored her son. She was tough and demanding.

"My mom to this day is the hardest coach I've ever had," Zion said. "There were times when my stepdad would look at me and say, 'You had a good game' and my mom would be like, 'I don't know what you're talking about, you had two or three turn-overs.'"

That was Sharonda Sampson. She saw great things in her boy and would do anything for him, but he was also going to have to do plenty for himself. There would be no excuses.

"How would I describe her? Tough love," Zion said. "She would always be the first one to keep it real with me . . . She taught me growing up [that] whenever I needed something, she would do every-thing in her power just to get it for me. She put aside her dreams. I don't think a lot of people are fortu-nate enough to be in that kind of situation, so I just thank God that I got a mother like I did."

Here's where another secret weapon comes in: Zion's mind.

Zion was a good student. He did well in his classes at Johnakin. He often helped his friends when they needed it. So when he graduated from middle school, he got an amazing offer: an academic scholarship to Spartanburg Day School, about two hundred miles away, in Spartanburg, South Carolina.

Spartanburg Day has a really nice campus, with crisply mowed grass and a big building with bright white pillars. It looked more like a college than any school Zion was used to—he hadn't yet seen the school buildings he would someday walk into at Duke.

Spartanburg Day even had a cool, unique mascot called the Griffin, which is kind of a mix between an eagle and a lion. That would kind of fit, right? Zion could soar like an eagle, but he was also strong like a lion. Zion knew he would love being a Griffin.

So what's Spartanburg, South Carolina, like? If you've ever eaten at a Denny's restaurant, you've had a taste of Spartanburg. Denny's was founded in California, but its headquarters are in Spartanburg. If you've ever taken a ride in a BMW, you have had a hint of Spartanburg. The BMW factory in nearby

Greer chugs out more than a thousand cars and SUVs a day. And if you happen to be in Spartanburg in the late summer, there's a chance you'll run into one of the Carolina Panthers, since the team holds its annual preseason training camp there. Everyone from former quarterback Cam Newton to running back Christian McCaffrey has practiced in Spartanburg.

"It's almost midway between Atlanta and Charlotte," said Eric Boynton, sports editor at the Spartanburg *Herald-Journal*. "It's one of those small, sleepy Southern towns."

Some rising hoops stars choose to go to high school in big cities like New York or Los Angeles, where the spotlight will be on them. And others transfer to basketball-famous academies like Oak Hill in Virginia or Montverde in Florida. But Zion's family moved into a quiet neighborhood in Spartanburg so he could attend a top academic school. As always, education came first.

The one-story, light-colored house had a white mailbox out front and a little overhang in the driveway to shelter the family car. Zion and his younger brother, Noah, would hang out in the driveway or practice taking shots at the hoop around the side of the house. One of Zion's favorite things to do, even to this day, is play with Noah. They're more than ten years apart in age, but they are buddies for life.

When Zion and his family got to Spartanburg, his basketball future was not at all clear. He wasn't going to any kind of basketball factory. Spartanburg Day was a kindergarten-through-twelfth-grade school, and there would be fewer than fifty kids in Zion's class when he started ninth grade there. The school didn't even have a full-time hoops coach. Zion's new coach, Lee Sartor, was a police officer as his main job. There were no expectations of winning state championships.

And most surprising of all, Zion still hadn't been that tall in eighth grade. He was five-eleven. Tall for his age, but not tall by basketball standards.

But between eighth and ninth grades, Zion had a major growth spurt. By the time he walked into high school at Spartanburg Day for the first time, he would be almost six foot four, and his whole life would completely change.

In the words of Psalm 48:2, "Beautiful in elevation, the joy of the whole earth, is Mount Zion."

Zion was about to elevate in a whole new way.

3
AAU

ZION WILLIAMSON could not dunk.

Imagine that.

He tried and tried, but he couldn't do it.

Pretty much every Zion fan on the planet has seen him dunk, whether in person, on TV, or online. Zion is *known* for dunking.

But there he was, soon to be a high school freshman at Spartanburg Day, and Zion Williamson couldn't dunk.

Now, not every future basketball star is able to dunk before the end of middle school, but a lot of them can. LeBron James first dunked in eighth grade. It was in a students-vs.-teachers game. LeBron got a steal, took off down the court, lifted off, and sent it down. The other students went nuts. One of the teachers was so excited, he unbolted the rim from the backboard and kept it as memorabilia.

As for Zion, well, he had to wait. What was the problem? he wondered. He was left-handed, so he tried to leap off his left foot. Nope. He tried off his right foot. Nope. He took a running start. Still, nothing seemed to work.

He spent a ton of time working on the rest of his game—shooting, dribbling, free throws, footwork—but boy, did he want to get that first dunk. Then he had an idea.

Maybe if he bounced the ball off the backboard, he wouldn't think so much about jumping. He could just focus on grabbing the ball and finding the rim.

So he tossed the ball off the glass, grabbed it . . . and dunked! By worrying a little less, he had accomplished a little more. It had worked.

There were so many dunks to come, but one in particular stood out even before Zion started at Spartanburg Day.

In 2013, Zion tried out for an Amateur Athletic

Union (AAU) travel team called the South Carolina Hornets. The team was already talented before he arrived. One of the Hornets' players, a kid a year older than Zion, wasn't sure if the younger kid would make it on the top team. He liked Zion, but he thought he might belong on the younger Hornets team.

Then he saw Zion do a windmill dunk and he knew Zion would be his teammate along with the older Hornets.

That new teammate's name? Ja Morant, who lived in Dalzell, South Carolina, a small town of about two thousand people. It was a little more than an hour away from where Zion went to middle school. Ja's full name was Temetrius Jamel Morant, but he went by "Ja," and just like Zion, his parents had been athletes. Ja's mom had played hoops and his dad had been a high school teammate of former NBA star Ray Allen.

South Carolina is kind of an unlikely place to meet another NBA-bound player. The state's population is about five million. Only forty-four people born in South Carolina have ever made it to the NBA. You might recognize a few of them: Kevin Garnett was born in Greenville; Alex English was born in Columbia; Khris Middleton was born in Charleston.

But there they were, Zion and Ja, two kids who would, years later, reach the NBA. Neither knew it at the time, though. Neither was even considered the best player on the Hornets.

"Me and Ja were role players," Zion said on the podcast of NBA veteran player J.J. Redick. "What people don't know is there's a dude who [went] to [the University of Mississippi], Devontae Shuler. In South Carolina, he was the guy. I remember I used to play with him. I'm playing up an age group. I'm like, 'Man this dude is going coast-to-coast finishing. Pulling up for transition threes like he's [Steph] Curry.' I'm like, 'I'm just a ninth grader.' He was like top 30 in the nation. A certified bucket."

Zion was being a little humble in that interview, but Devontae Shuler was quite confident and the bigger prospect at the time. Devontae would often tell people to "Remember our faces!" Remember they would.

Overshadowed by Devontae, Zion and Ja became good friends. Zion would later make his number 12 jersey famous at Spartanburg Day, but on this Hornets team, it was Ja who wore that number. "He was the ultimate warrior," said Ricky Taylor, the Hornets' coach, of Ja. "Slender and small but so tough. He got banged up but always got back up."

Zion took number 32. While he'd end up wearing a different number down the line, at that time he was already sporting his signature haircut, a flat-top style. Guess who would cut Zion's hair every now and then? It was Ja's dad, who was a barber.

"Our whole team was really close," said Coach Taylor. "They were definitely close. We had eight kids on that team. [Zion and Ja] were both laid-back kids. They didn't talk a lot. Both were basketball fanatics. They always said [basketball] was what they were going to do."

Coach Taylor remembers that in all his years of coaching, teams have played video games on bus rides and plane rides to tournaments. But not that year. With Zion and Ja leading the way, the boys just wanted to talk about basketball, watch basketball, and play basketball. So they weren't too tough to motivate. Taylor says now that he hardly had to coach the boys at all—especially because Ja's dad was his assistant coach, so basketball was always on their minds.

That year the Hornets started up in March and

played through August, mostly on weekends and with breaks during periods to work around the school year. The Hornets would always play older teams—kids as old as eleventh graders.

"We won most of 'em," said Coach Taylor.

Zion and Ja had fun, but they knew they were there to develop as players first.

"Their priorities stayed in line," Coach Taylor said. "They never put anything bad in their body. They really focused on eating right."

As that season went on, fans at other games at the same gym would often wander over to the Hornets' court. Word spread about the three young kids—Zion, Ja, and Devontae—on the eight-player team that was beating older clubs. During one game in North Carolina, the fans who watched Zion got a real treat.

The Hornets were playing a team sponsored by Nike. At one point during the game, an opposing player went on a fast break; he didn't see anyone around, so he assumed he was about to cruise in for an easy layup.

Out of nowhere came number 32, the lefty with a big leap. Zion rose from the court and pinned the Nike player's shot against the backboard with both hands. He came down with the ball in his grasp—a block and a rebound in one thunderous moment.

"I was . . . wow," Coach Taylor said, remembering the play years later.

But there was a whistle. The referee called a foul. The Nike player went to the line as the crowd kept buzzing and the Hornets looked around quizzically.

A few minutes later, the referee walked over to Coach Taylor.

"That wasn't a foul," he confessed to Coach Taylor. "The whistle was in my mouth and I just blew it."

The official was so stunned that he called an incorrect foul!

"Zion's athletic ability," said Coach Taylor, "his size, his IQ. He made the game look so simple."

Zion and Ja wouldn't play on the same team again after that season. Ja was already in high school in Sumter, South Carolina, and he would struggle to get a lot of attention from colleges. He later received a scholarship to play ball at a small university in Kentucky called Murray State. Ja only got that scholarship offer because he happened to be playing in a tournament where a Murray State assistant coach was scouting a different player on a different team. When the assistant got hungry, he went to get a snack and walked past a court where Ja was playing right as Ja made some incredible play. Just like that, the assistant began scouting Ja.

Still, despite their limited playing time together, Zion would always be a huge fan of Ja. One night in early 2016, a few months after their time as teammates ended, a video was posted to Twitter of Ja going up for a dunk. Ja couldn't quite throw it down and Zion posted "Almost." That only got seven retweets, since in those days they didn't have many followers. Ja saw the tweet later and wrote back to Zion, "trying to get like you" with a laughing emoji. Even though they were no longer teammates, they still remained supportive of each other from a distance.

A month after that, Ja posted some of his highlights on Twitter. Not a ton of people noticed. Zion jumped right in like a proud younger brother, boosting the highlights with his own post: "Check out my boy highlights #youcantguardhim."

Eventually people would realize Zion knew what he was talking about. In June of 2019, the NBA held its annual draft. With a ton of elite players to choose from, Zion went first to New Orleans. Who came next up, at number two? Zion's old teammate, Ja Morant. The two old friends hugged each other and celebrated their long journeys. They'd begun as backup AAU players and now suddenly they were standing on the center stage of the NBA draft. It was only the second time in NBA history that two players from the same state went first and second.

Not bad for a couple of South Carolina kids.

4

Spartanburg

ZION GRABBED jersey number 12 for the Griffins of Spartanburg Day, and there would be many highlights in that uniform over the next four years. However, there was a definite lowlight right at the beginning of his Spartanburg Day career: He fell and broke his wrist during a game.

Zion went to get some X-rays, and the doctor examined the slides. There was bad news—the break was confirmed—but there was good, though surprising, news as well: the doctor discovered that Zion's growth plate was open.

What did that mean? Well, it meant Zion was growing fast, and that he might grow as much as another five inches—and soon!

That was big news to a kid who wanted to play college basketball and possibly even make it to the NBA. He hadn't been even six feet tall in eighth grade, and only a few months later he was dunking. Now the doctor said he'd only get taller.

There would be growing pains, though—literally. Zion grew so fast that his knees began to hurt a lot. Sharonda would spend some nights after school helping her son ice his legs to ease the soreness.

It wasn't just his height that changed; it was his overall size. Lots of kids grow tall and pretty much all elite basketball players are tall, but Zion was *big*. He would grow to look more like a linebacker than a small forward. LeBron James is considered a once-in-a-generation player at six foot eight, 250 pounds. That's roughly the same weight as NBA star Giannis Antetokounmpo and NFL stars Cam Newton and Khalil Mack. But Zion would grow to a whopping 285 pounds. That would one day make him one of the heaviest players in the NBA.

And when you think "heavy" you don't think "hops." Most people who weigh nearly three hundred pounds are ground-bound by all that gravity. But not Zion. No, Zion would have *power*. Those growing pains that required ice from his mom would build his legs into launching pads. By the time he got to college, Zion had a forty-five-inch vertical jump. That's three and three quarters feet in the air.

Thanks to his size and athleticism, Zion would spend his high school years evolving into a basketball force the likes of which few had seen before. Remember: His mother had been a leaper on her college track team, and his biological father had been a fierce pass rusher. Put those two qualities together and what do you get? A once-in-a-generation talent.

There was also a matter of his training. Because he'd been relatively small in middle school, Zion had learned to play guard, where ball handling, decision making, and outside shooting were key skills.

"He was taught that at that time because of his size," Lee Anderson, Zion's stepdad, said. "By the time the summer [after eighth grade] was over, Zion was six-four."

Once his broken wrist healed, Zion turned into a sort-of superhero who didn't know his own strength. Anderson was convinced that in Zion he had a special talent on his hands.

"[My stepdad] said, 'By your junior or senior year you will be the number-1 player in the country,'" Zion said in the mini-documentary *Zion*. "I said, 'Okay, come on now, let's be a little realistic. Come back to reality. I'm not even ranked now, I'm not on anybody's radar.'"

He would be soon enough. The bigger he got, the harder it was to miss him.

In an interview with *GQ* magazine, Zion explained his surprise at his growth: "I didn't pick up all this weight until junior year. Freshman year, I was small. I was six-three, 175—like, I was *small*. And over the course of about two years, I picked up a hundred pounds. I mean, I would look at myself and go, *Wow, I'm 250!*"

When he got even bigger over the next couple of years, a newspaper reporter from *The Wall Street Journal* asked a physicist to estimate the force of taking a charge from Zion. The answer: like being hit by a jeep going ten miles an hour. Another reporter from the New Orleans site NOLA.com asked a physiology expert from Louisiana State University to figure out how much energy was produced when Zion jumped. The expert said Zion's leaps would generate ten thousand watts of energy—enough to power a hundred-watt light bulb for four days.

At first, not many people around the country noticed Zion's ability to levitate through the air like he had a jetpack on. But one exception was videographer Bryce Lanning. Lanning ran a company called EliteMixtapes, and he looked for high school athletes to film for YouTube highlights. Lanning, who lives in Charlotte, North Carolina, saw Zion play and immediately believed he had stumbled onto someone special. Before Zion's junior year, Lanning wrote to Zion and asked permission to come film his games. Zion said yes.

Over the next year, Lanning repeatedly made the hour-plus drive from Charlotte to Spartanburg to film Zion and then posted his highlights on YouTube.

Right away he noticed something very different about Zion's dunks. Most of the fierce dunks in high school created a *ka-thunk* sound as the rim reacted to the force of the dunk.

Zion's dunks, however, "sounded like a gunshot."

Lanning is used to high school stars making it look easy because they're simply better than everyone else out there. But Zion, he realized, was on a whole different level.

"I saw players who were scared of him," Lanning

said. "Players would start to back up when he came at them. They didn't want anything to do with him."

Zion's highlights made for terrific footage. As Lanning or his business partner, Dex, posted videos following Zion's games, fans would tune in almost as soon as the video went live.

"It was as if people were waiting up late to see the highlights," Lanning said.

Before too long, it felt like the whole world was watching Zion. Some of the YouTube videos got more than a million views.

One standout moment occurred in December of Zion's junior year. When a pass came in from the three-point line, Zion decided to not only try to catch it, but also to windmill it through the net. By then his wingspan—the distance from the fingertips on one hand to the fingertips on the other when the arms are held horizontal to the floor—was closing in on seven feet, so when he swooped the ball around and down, he looked almost like a velociraptor coming in from the sky. This was in a road game for Spartanburg Day, and when he nailed that windmill alley-oop slam, even the opposing fans roared.

Only a couple of months later, Zion did something even more stunning. He wanted to try a

360-degree windmill dunk. That meant leaping into the air, rotating his entire body, reaching back with the ball, and then dunking it. That's the kind of move you only see in an NBA slam-dunk contest.

Unless, that is, you're Zion Williamson.

Zion had first tried—and failed to execute—the move in a game in February 2017. But in the next game, on the campus of Wofford College, he got free at half-court and built up some momentum on the race to the basket. Along the way, he made up his mind: He was going to try it again. He jumped, spun, reached, came around, and *slammed* it home.

The building erupted! One of his teammates was so psyched that he bounced high into the air as if he was about to dunk an imaginary basketball. When Zion landed, he turned toward center court and screamed in excitement.

The dunk was so crazy that ESPN's *SportsCenter* put the footage on Twitter, and thousands of people shared it.

Pretty impressive for a kid who hadn't been able to dunk just three years earlier.

5

Stardom

IN SOUTH CAROLINA, sports fans are obsessed with football. The state is home to two powerhouse college football programs, Clemson and the University of South Carolina. And on the professional side, NFL teams from neighboring states, the Carolina Panthers and Atlanta Falcons, also receive a ton of love.

Yet from 2016 to 2018, South Carolina sports fans were scouring the Internet to look up the schedule for the Spartanburg Day boys' basketball team.

Suddenly, a high school hoops team's game was the toughest ticket to get.

Everyone wanted to see Zion—even if they weren't normally fans of high school basketball. Opposing teams brought extra spectators to Zion's home games. Fans of college teams wore their gear to the Spartanburg gym in the hopes that Zion would choose their favorite school. Pretty much everyone had a phone out, hoping to capture the next Zion highlight, ready to share it on social media and watch it go viral.

With all those eyes on him, Zion was always ready to put on a show.

"He wasn't afraid to miss an overly ambitious dunk," said Eric Boynton of the Spartanburg *Herald-Journal*. "He was known to do dunk-contest stuff even in games. And I never saw him miss a dunk."

Yet once people entered the gym and took their seats—or perhaps stood for the whole game—they saw a more complete player than the dunk highlights showed. Zion had been practicing everything, not just alley-oops. He played with a controlled fury, dancing around opponents and rushing up the court.

"When I saw his handles," Lanning said, "I thought, 'Well this is scary.'"

His passes sometimes looked like lasers, as he

would reach back and fire the ball to a cutting team-mate on a fast break. In the low post, he could spin and shake off defenders. He could dribble like a point guard and rebound like a center.

It wasn't just fans who took note. Basketball experts were in on him, too. At a young age, Zion was already showing qualities that were extremely rare.

"When you see him in transition, he could cock back his arm as he jumps—like LeBron does," said Justin Zormelo, who has helped train NBA stars Paul George and Kevin Durant. "He can do it left-handed, but he does it right-handed. You can't name me one player in the NBA who can cock back like that with his off hand. It's not looking like it's his off hand. This kid comes down in traffic and raises up with the opposite hand. That tells you he's a different athlete. You could think he's right-handed [even though he's left-handed]."

Zormelo noticed something else, too: Zion didn't use all his power on the first jump. He could jump nearly as high if he missed and took another shot.

"He'll get to the square on the second jump," he said. "He could shoot a shot in the paint [the area around the basket], get his own rebound, and dunk with power and height."

Some of that is raw strength, which is genetics and growth. Most high schoolers don't have that strength. But there is another ingredient, too: agility. He was able to overpower smaller players without just crashing into them and getting called for a foul, although sometimes he got called without even bumping the opponent.

"I'm very mobile, and I think I'm nimble," Zion said in an interview with *GQ*. "I can get from spot to spot real quick. But, you know, the fact that I'm so much stronger, when I attack the basket, when I get fouled, a regular foul would not faze me much because I would just power through it."

Zion needed a strong core to stay in control not only in the paint but in the air. It's one of the most important strengths a big man can have—core strength.

"Michael Jordan was agile in the air," said Zormelo. "He has a strong core. People just look at him as a jumper, and he jumps high. No, he had control of his body from a young age. That's not from lifting weights. You can't just be a genetic freak. Something happened to make him strong in the middle."

Oh, and then there was Zion's defense. Zion was like a brick wall with spires on top. He came out of nowhere, swatting shots out of the air and sending a message warning about the next drive into the lane. One of his most famous high school moments came when he leaped so high to block a shot against the glass with both hands that he appeared to slam his head against the side of the backboard and tumble to the hardwood below.

All of that natural ability was honed with hours of tough practices, workouts, and trying to eat healthy. Even someone as gifted as Zion can't rely on athletic ability alone. It was about maximizing what he had while learning *how* to play the game.

"He was so fundamentally sound," said Zion's AAU coach, Ricky Taylor. "He could do it all. Great dribbler, passer, rebounder. He never really took a bad shot."

There was one more way Zion developed as a player and person during his high school years: by sharpening his mind.

Zion always wanted to be a complete basketball player and a complete student. He appreciated all the love he got from fans for his dunking ability, but he didn't like being known solely for his dunks. He was bothered that people were more interested in seeing him compete in a dunk contest than in an actual game. Sometimes, when teammates started dunking in pregame drills, he would decide to simply lay the ball into the hoop instead.

"So people want to classify me as a dunker, they can," he told *GQ*. "If my opponent wants to think of me as a dunker, it's just gonna shock them more when I show them another part of my game."

It motivated him to become a complete player and increase his basketball IQ. But Zion exercised his mind in many different ways, on and off the court, during high school. For instance, he enjoyed writing poetry.

He took a creative writing course at Spartanburg Day, and he was one of fewer than ten students in the class. A man named Bill Pell taught Zion, and he told ESPN that Zion's poems were "remarkable." Zion was shy about reading his poems aloud in class, and he was shy about sharing them, but he had a knack for it.

Zion wasn't so shy on the court, yet at the same time he didn't hog the spotlight. He was at a tiny school and he seemed comfortable there. A lot of high school basketball stars want the limelight and all the attention. Zion wasn't really like that. Sometimes he even blended into the flow of the game a little too much, and his Spartanburg Day coach had to tell him to take over.

"I appreciate that people . . . give me the comparisons to LeBron, but I'm not LeBron," Zion told *GQ*. "I'm myself. Before I got big, I was playing point guard, so I'm kinda like a pass-first person. Some people tell me I should be more selfish, but that's not me."

In the middle of his junior year, Zion's team faced a big challenge: a tournament game against Gray Collegiate Academy and its top high school prospect, Jalek Felton. The line to see that game stretched out the gym doors and into the parking lot.

"That game—it was electric," said Gray coach Dion Bethea. "It was so loud. Everybody was trying to get in. We had a really good team. But Zion was a one-man show."

The one-man show began even before the game. Zion threw down some forceful dunks in warm-ups, with each one leading to shouts of "Whoa!" from the fans already standing in the bleachers.

Coach Bethea was no slouch. He had played against Hall of Famer Ray Allen in high school, and over the coming years he would lead Gray to several state titles.

But he had never seen anyone like Zion.

His strategy was simple: Keep him away from the rim. "We have to make him shoot the basketball," he said. "I really wanted to try to make him shoot the basketball. It didn't go well."

Bryce Lanning from EliteMixtapes was there, and he set up along the baseline. It was smart to start filming early, because right off the opening tip, an alley-oop pass arced toward the left side of the backboard.

"I thought it was too high," Bethea recalled.

It wasn't. Zion soared toward the goal, grabbed the ball, and dunked.

The crowd went berserk. The game was already off the chain.

"He's a dog," Bethea said. "When he wanted to get to that basket, he could."

Coach Bethea tried different tactics. Nothing worked. Zion scored 53 points that day. Gray scored 53 points as a team.

And after the final buzzer? Zion made sure to say "Good game" to his opponents and sign autographs for fans.

"He didn't come off as an arrogant guy," said

Bethea. "He's not a kid who felt he had already arrived. I wouldn't be surprised if one day they named the gym after him. He's a great kid."

After that performance, things got really wild for Zion. Soon, the famous rapper Drake posted a photo of himself wearing a Spartanburg Day number 12 jersey on Instagram. Zion couldn't believe it. He was just a high school kid, after all.

"I had hundreds of messages—group chats, like 50 Snapchat notifications. My phone just blew up," Zion told *SLAM* magazine. "They were all like, go check Instagram, look what Drake just posted. I saw that he had my jersey on, and I sent him an IG message that said, 'Thanks for showing me so much love—I don't think you understand how much this means to me. You're my favorite rapper.'"

You might expect someone's ego to grow after receiving all that attention. (Even NFL wide receiver Odell Beckham Jr. posted a pic of himself wearing Zion's number.) But not Zion. He would sometimes scream after a big dunk, or he could play physical, but he didn't shove anyone or embarrass anyone. He didn't taunt or showboat.

"He's not mean to [other] kids," said Zormelo.

"He's obviously bigger, stronger, faster. He might humiliate them, but he does it only in the spirit of the game. That shows so much."

Certainly, nobody is perfect, but Zion seemed to stay humble even as he went from an eighth grader who couldn't dunk to an Instagram sensation who counted celebrities as fans. He probably could have dunked on just about every play, but he liked setting up his teammates and he liked playing guard and forward. He could have walked up the court every time, but he hustled and he worked hard.

And he treated fans with respect. He remembered patiently waiting as a kid to get autographs from his favorite high school players. So when he got to high school, he made sure to wait after every game—home or road—to sign for young fans. The Griffins' bus back to school would have to wait for Zion's signing line to end before leaving.

"When I was a little kid, even though I didn't know what advanced dunks were—like windmills, 360s—I used to just want to see somebody dunk. Like, 'Can you dunk? Dunk it!'" Zion said in his interview with *SLAM*. "So when I see little kids go, 'Zion, dunk it!' I just look at them and say, 'I got you.'"

One time Spartanburg Day hosted a dunk contest and Zion was a guest judge. Before too long, fans started to chant his name. They wanted Zion to throw one down. After a few minutes, Zion grabbed a basketball, walked out to center court, and began dribbling. The crowd began to whoop as Zion approached the basket and lobbed the ball against the glass backboard. He grabbed the orange orb, windmilled, and slammed it home. He hadn't even removed the backpack hooked around his shoulders.

"It's refreshing to see," said Zormelo. "People in our [older] generation can't say anything bad about the kid. He's playing the right way. He says the right things. He's not selfish."

As a sophomore, Zion led his Spartanburg Day team to a state championship and all of the Griffins celebrated together at the Beacon Drive-In. It's a cool spot with a long, shiny counter and tasty menu options like Chili Cheeseburger a'Plenty—which means it comes with fries and onion rings. The next season, as a junior, Zion averaged an astounding 36.8 points and 13.0 rebounds per game, and the Griffins repeated as champions. Then, in his senior year, Spartanburg Day did it again.

Still, despite the three state championships and

his growing fame, Zion spent a lot of time at home, hanging out with his little brother, Noah. He was still a "homebody," according to Sharonda, happy to be in a smaller group.

But the world was watching. And everyone knew he was headed to bigger places.

The only question was . . . where?

"Zion's got eight points in the last minute."

"They want Zion to get it."

"BLOCKED IT!"

6

College Recruitment

YOU MIGHT THINK the number-1 college recruit in the nation would be the six-foot-six, 265-pound dunking machine with Saran Wrap defense and silky ball-handling skills. You might guess the number-1 recruit in the nation would be Zion Williamson.

Guess again.

It was RJ Barrett.

Who was RJ? He was actually raised in Canada, and then he moved to Florida to play at top basketball academy Montverde. He was so good that he was technically the top player in two different classes. He was originally scheduled to graduate from high school in 2019, but since he felt he was ready for college basketball sooner and he had gotten ahead academically, he switched and reclassified into the Class of 2018. He was still ranked number 1. And the college basketball world agreed: RJ got scholarship offers from Arizona, Duke, Indiana, Kansas, Kentucky, Texas, UCLA, and many other powerhouse teams.

RJ could do it all: He was about as tall as Zion; he was fast; he could shoot, pass, rebound, and defend. He was rated the best high school player in the country by 247Sports, Rivals, and ESPN.

It made a lot of sense that RJ was ranked so high. In 2017, he played in the FIBA Basketball World Cup, a major international hoops tournament. As a Canadian, he was matched up against the American team, which was coached by one of college basketball's most famous coaches, the University of Kentucky's John Calipari. Unfazed, Canada beat Team USA, with RJ having an outstanding performance with 38 points. He led the Canadians to a gold medal in that event, averaging 21.6 points per game.

Zion never played in a FIBA tournament. And he never played for a basketball-player factory like

Montverde. He stayed local, in South Carolina, and played all four years for Spartanburg Day—a school that had 450 students, including preschoolers, and no football team.

Talent scouts who ranked players were used to seeing high school stars playing against other high school stars. But Zion hadn't faced that type of competition regularly, so it was tough to figure out how good he actually was. Yes, he was dominating every game, but he was dominating players who weren't close to his level. When Zion burst onto the social media scene with an alley-oop dunk that caused fans to pour out of the stands and a referee to shoo them back off the court, he was only fifteen years old and the seventeenth-ranked player in his class.

There was another minor concern: In 2017, the same year RJ was turning heads at the FIBA tournament, Zion was recovering from a slight knee injury. He missed some playing time as a precaution, and although the knee would be just fine, he lost some chances to prove his status as one of the top high school players in America.

Don't think Zion was ignored or overlooked. During the summers, he attended national talent camps put on by shoe companies and competed at the highest level of AAU basketball with his travel team. He may not have played at that level during the high school season, but at one point or another, he faced off against all the best players his age. And when the city of Spartanburg hosted a show-case tournament featuring its hometown hero, so many college coaches flew in on private jets that the local airport nearly ran out of room to park all the planes.

Zion made All-State as a freshman, but didn't receive any college offers, like top recruits often do. That changed after his sophomore year, when South Carolina schools like Wofford and Clemson said they wanted him to play for them. Then after he played well in a tournament, he got a scholarship offer from Iowa State, which is located nowhere near South Carolina. It was then that he knew he was going to have some schools to choose from.

He just didn't know yet how many choices he'd have.

It wouldn't be long before the craziness set in. His mom had to lay down the law. Soon, so many college coaches were trying to get ahold of Zion, she insisted on no texts or calls after 10 P.M.

Before long, most of the giants of college hoops

wanted Zion to play for them. The University of North Carolina's Roy Williams, one of the top coaches in the country, said Zion had talent comparable to that of a former Tar Heel named Michael Jordan. John Calipari, known for putting together loaded teams at Kentucky, showed strong interest. At one point, for the first time ever, Spartanburg Day had to charge money for tickets to basketball games because there were so many fans who wanted to see not only Zion, but all the big-time coaches who flocked to the stands. (One fan even drove down from Maine!)

The attention paid to Zion and his recruitment was so insane that a family friend and former security guard had to keep his eye on the teenager, just to make sure no one bothered him too much. It felt like everyone was obsessed with his college choice, forgetting that he was still a teenager—still without a driver's license, still spending his downtime watching *Dragon Ball Z* and playing Connect 4.

Where did Zion want to play college hoops? Turns out he wasn't quite sure.

"I'm looking at the school that has a bigger plan for me once I finish with basketball," he told *The Charlotte Observer*. "I want to go to a coach who has my best interests [at heart]. And I want to go to a school with strong academics."

This gave out-of-state schools like Duke and North Carolina a shot at Zion, but for many months it seemed like in-state schools had the lead.

A lot of people in South Carolina wanted Zion to "stay home" and represent the Palmetto State in college. The University of South Carolina had coach Frank Martin, an intense former schoolteacher who was high on discipline. Zion showed up at a Gamecocks game and little kids lined up in the aisles to high-five him or ask for an autograph during timeouts. The idea of Zion playing college nearby captivated so many of them.

Clemson had a huge advantage: Zion's stepfather had played basketball there. Spartanburg wasn't that far from Clemson, either. Throughout most of Zion's recruitment, Lee Anderson thought Clemson was in the front seat. Anderson didn't want to be too pushy, though. It had to be Zion's decision.

There was still that one misconception that followed Zion throughout his high school career: that he was all about the dunks. Zion wanted these coaches to realize he was a student of the entire sport.

Zion would watch NBA and college games any chance he could. He wasn't just a fan, either. He tried to study how the great ones played, especially when they didn't have the ball. His mother suggested he go one step further and watch some of the NBA's all-time best players of the 1980s and 1990s. Maybe he could learn from them.

"It was my mom that led me to watching Michael Jordan and the [1990s] Bulls," Zion said. "I asked her, when I first started playing basketball, 'Who should I go watch?' And she told me, 'Jordan, [Larry] Bird, and Magic [Johnson].' I watched—I think I started with Magic. I was like, 'Man, he can pass the ball.' And Bird, you know, he can shoot. He's an all-around player.

"But when I got to Jordan, she told me to watch full games, not highlights," Zion continued. "And I watched full games [of all] the stuff he was doing. It was incredible to watch, getting a steal, saving it, and then doing a backwards layup or floating through the lane, like through three people, dunking it. So as a kid, that really caught my attention, and from then, I just watched every full-game Michael Jordan clip I could find."

He wanted to be a complete player, which was

why it was reassuring that he garnered interest from the legendary program at Duke University: Coach Mike Krzyzewski was the winningest coach in the history of college basketball, and he would never want to bring in a player who only dunked. If Zion chose to commit to Duke, he knew he'd be in for much more than just TV exposure.

Though Zion had 1.7 million Instagram followers while still in high school, most people had never seen him play a full game on TV, so they didn't realize how good he actually was. Zion still had something to prove as a basketball player, and playing on a big collegiate stage at Duke or Kentucky or North Carolina could do that.

Still, there was a general belief around Spartanburg that Zion would choose Clemson. Eric Boynton of the Spartanburg *Herald-Journal* arrived at Zion's announcement press conference expecting to write a column about what Zion's commitment would do for the Tigers, which rarely had a good team. For a program like Clemson's, beating out all the elite schools and landing Zion would have been huge.

"I thought for sure he was going to Clemson," Boynton said. "This might be the kid that has so much confidence and ability—he might be the one that changes things around there. Clemson had a pretty veteran team. He'd have experience around him. He'd be legendary even if he played one year."

Zion made his college announcement on his mom's birthday, and that was not a coincidence. It was Sharonda who'd been Zion's first coach. It was Sharonda who'd given him his jumping genes. It was Sharonda who'd made sure Zion worked early in the morning and late at night, who'd made sure Zion went to a good high school, and made sure Zion shut off his phone at 10 P.M. even when important coaches were calling.

It's easy to go astray when you're famous, when everyone is trying to get something from you, and when millions of dollars in salary and endorsements are only a couple of years away. Sharonda had worked hard to keep Zion on track and humble.

The Spartanburg Day gymnasium was packed on that fateful Saturday night. It was another memorable moment for a football town that suddenly had gone crazy over a local basketball player. "You don't see that kind of buzz in our area," Boynton said. "You don't have a Deshaun Watson or a Trevor Lawrence from one of our local schools."

Zion hid the cap from the school of his choice under a table. The color of the cap was Duke blue.

Attracted by the school's legendary coach, top-notch academics, and historic basketball legacy, Zion would be moving back to North Carolina, where Duke was located. The state where his mom had played college sports and given birth to a boy she named after a mountain.

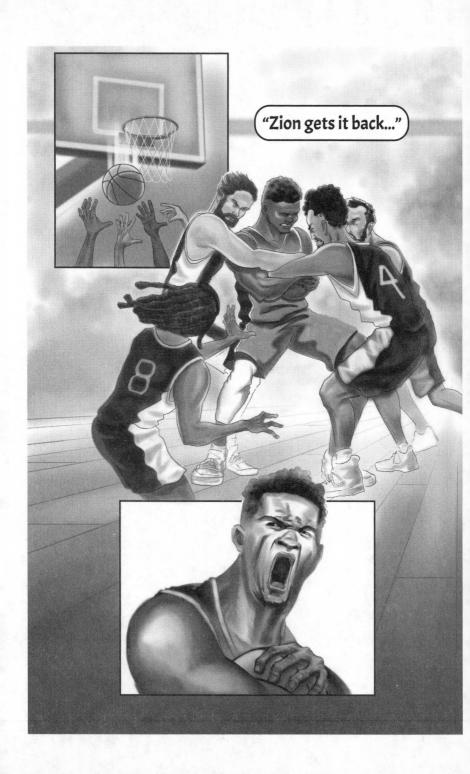

7

Duke

DUKE IS ONE OF THE BEST universities in America, with about 6,500 undergraduate students, and beginning in the summer of 2018, that number included a big kid who had grown up in little old Florence, South Carolina. The university has produced fourteen billionaires, one president (Richard Nixon), and one incredible basketball program under coach Mike Krzyzewski.

Coach K, as he's known, has won more college basketball games than any coach in history. He took over at Duke in 1980 and has led the Blue Devils to five national titles. He was also the head coach of the United States national team, where he led NBA greats such as Kobe Bryant, LeBron James, and Kevin Durant to gold medals in the 2008, 2012, and 2016 Olympics.

"Coach K, he's just the most legendary coach to ever coach college basketball," Zion said. "That's why I feel like players come to Duke, they have a winning history. You want to be part of a great season."

Duke plays in Cameron Indoor Stadium, which seats 9,300 fans and is located in the middle of campus. Unlike most schools, Duke reserves the best seats in the stadium for its students, who are known as the Cameron Crazies. They are famous for standing and screaming during the entire game and coming up with creative ways to distract opposing players.

So many Duke students want to attend the basketball games that back in the 1980s, a tradition began in which students camp outside Cameron the night before tickets go on sale, hoping to be first in line. Instead of staying in their nice dorm rooms, they choose tents, sleeping bags, and flashlights. Coach K used to come by with pizza for everyone.

Soon there were so many tents that the area became known as Krzyzewskiville, or K-ville.

The K-ville fans have seen some incredible players through the years, including nine who were named National Player of the Year. Zion wanted to be number ten.

But Duke isn't the only show in town. The university is located in Durham, North Carolina, which is part of the region called the Research Triangle. It also includes the cities of Raleigh, home to North Carolina State University, and Chapel Hill, where the University of North Carolina (UNC) is located.

All three schools have not just top academic programs, but also top basketball teams. Each has won the national title and all have fierce rivalries with each other. The one between Duke and UNC is especially intense.

In selecting Duke, Zion chose the spotlight and the expectations that came with it. He knew all eyes would be on him and the goal would be to win a national title. Anything less would be a disappointment for the Blue Devils. Nearly every game would be on national TV and his performances would be analyzed and picked apart. This was the big leagues.

All that winning meant there were a lot of Duke

fans out there. It also meant there were many more Duke haters who liked to cheer against the Blue Devils. Anywhere Duke went, there were going to be people hoping for their failure. To be a Blue Devil was to embrace that.

"Just be glad you are in a position where people notice you," Coach K said he tells his players of the jeers and boos they receive. "That reaction from fans was built on years of great players and teams who came before. You are now part of something bigger than just you or this season's team."

Coach K attended the United States Military Academy at West Point and served as an officer in the Army before becoming a basketball coach. He still runs his program with the discipline of the military. Even in his seventies—he was seventy-one when Zion arrived on campus—he is demanding and can be unforgiving. Complete effort is expected during every moment of every practice, let alone in games. At the same time, he wants equal, if not even more, focus in the classroom.

Duke is not the place for the weak.

"A successful team has to have talent, of course," Coach K said. "It also has to have trust in one another and a commitment to one another. You can't just win with talent."

Part of building that trust and commitment came through practice and other duties that showed a responsibility to the team. Even great players were going to get yelled at. But the trade-off was obvious: Not only would Coach K make you the best player you could be, there was also a sense of accomplishment that came from playing for him. Former Duke players called it the Brotherhood. It didn't matter if the other guy was a teammate or had played decades before or after you; you were all brothers.

"The Brotherhood represents family," Zion said. "And I'm all about family."

Zion wasn't the only new member of the family in the Class of 2018. He was part of an incredible recruiting class, including two players that high school scouts had ranked above Zion.

RJ Barrett, the number-1 recruit in the country, was one of them. Then there was Cam Reddish, who stood six foot eight and came from the Philadelphia area. He was ranked as the second-best recruit in America. Zion was number 3.

It was the first time ever that a school signed

the nation's top three recruits in a single year. Additionally, the number-8 recruit in America, Tre Jones, a point guard from Minnesota, was also coming to campus. Finally, there was Joey Baker, a six-eight forward from Fayetteville, North Carolina, who was a top-50 player nationally. This was probably the best recruiting class in the history of college basketball.

"The freshmen," Coach K said, "are really good."

Through the years, Coach K had either coached or coached against thousands and thousands of players, including most of the very best players on earth.

He had never seen anyone like Zion Williamson.

"God is good," Coach K said. "And God gave him extraordinary ability but also extraordinary intelligence on how to use the ability, and a work ethic to blend the two. He's a magnificent athlete. People just look at it as jumping. His lateral movement and his ability to move with speed and change directions is phenomenal.

"He's one of a kind," Coach K continued. "He's just one of a kind, and he's going to keep getting better . . . You can't say he's like somebody, because he's not like anybody. He's like Zion . . . he's the best athlete that I've had a chance to coach at Duke."

Coach K wasn't there to just watch him and cheer like a fan when he delivered some crazy dunk, though. The goal wasn't just to use Zion to win games for Duke. It was to help Zion improve and reach his full potential.

"My thing is to coach him," Coach K said. "He came to Duke to be coached and learn. We cannot put a ceiling on him."

There was no questioning Zion's natural athletic ability. To be truly great, however, he needed to be more than just athletic. In high school he could catch a ball and either outleap or overpower any defender. No one could match him physically.

In college, he'd face much better, and often older, competition. The NBA would take things to yet another level. It was full of grown men who could challenge him physically. He couldn't just dunk it every time. If he was going to become a truly great player in the NBA, he needed to know when to pass, how to move without the ball, how to shoot better from deep, how to position and time himself on rebounds, and so many other things.

The work began immediately. There would be no summer vacation for the Blue Devils. Zion and his teammates arrived in Durham in July 2018 to prepare for the season, which included a three-game exhibition tour of Canada in August.

Part of the process of getting Zion and the other freshmen ready was teaching them how to be healthy. That included classes in how to train, how to lift weights, how to do preventive stretching, how to eat, and so on. It even focused on the importance of sleep. Maybe in high school you could survive despite eating fast food and staying up late. Not in the NBA.

Duke left nothing to chance. It had an actual program designed by school doctors, scientists, and professors called the Michael W. Krzyzewski Human Performance Laboratory or the K-Lab. Zion was run through a series of tests that included cardio, strength, conditioning, biomechanical, and even visual capabilities. This allowed the K-Lab folks to establish baseline figures they could test against as the season progressed.

This was exactly what Zion had wanted—a state-of-the-art program.

"This was a big part of the recruiting process," Zion said. "Because if you want a long career in the NBA, you have to take care of your body."

Before practice began, the Blue Devils went through a week of basketball that mirrored what they would experience at the NBA Draft Combine. This gave them a chance to become familiar with drills such as spot-up jump shots, shooting off the dribble, and time jump shots while on the move (a drill that tests how many shots they could get up in a set period), only without the pressure of NBA general managers and scouts watching.

Once actual practice began, Zion immediately recognized that he wasn't in high school anymore. The intensity was far higher. The focus on the smallest of mistakes was greater. And Coach K spent a lot of time discussing the mental part of the game, which largely boiled down to determining the smartest play in a given situation, which is often a pass, not a shot.

Then there were his teammates—in addition to the high-flying fellow freshmen such as RJ and Cam, there were a couple of juniors, including Jack White, a six-seven, 222-pound forward who hailed from a small town in Australia, and Javin DeLaurier, a six-ten, 238-pound forward from Virginia.

Neither player was as talented as Zion. Neither

was a starter. But since they were both so respected for how hard they played in practice and in their limited game time, they were named team co-captains.

Both were also very strong and very physical. Zion couldn't just knock those guys out of the way every time. Or when he did, they'd be quick to get up and do the same in return. They weren't afraid to hammer his shoulders, push him out of the way, or throw their bodies into him. In fact, Coach K encouraged it. The tougher they made it for Zion in practice, the tougher Zion would get. And so these two played rough.

"I was actually very surprised at what a graceful athlete he is," Javin said of Zion. "You see all the YouTube highlights and all the stuff that he can do, but his footwork, his body control, and his skill set [are] really incredible. Going up against him every day has really been a challenge, but it's been really fun. I've enjoyed it."

It's said that champions are made by the work that gets done when no one is looking. Zion wasn't alone in the Duke practice gym, of course. His teammates and coaches were there, working just as hard.

But it was a long way from national television or

even Instagram Live. Day after day across that hot North Carolina summer, Zion battled to improve his game and his team.

The real action—and a shot at the national championship—was just around the corner.

8

Freshman Year

ONCE DUKE SIGNED the top-three high school players in America, anticipation skyrocketed for the 2018–19 season. It wasn't just Blue Devil fans, either. Everyone wanted to see these young stars play together. That meant a lot of eyes on Zion, who was no longer just a high school kid dunking on Instagram or playing in low-intensity All-Star games. This was a chance to see what he could really do against serious competition.

The NCAA allows college teams to take one

trip outside of the country every four years. The summer of 2018 was Duke's turn, and they scheduled three games in Canada, two in suburban Toronto and one in Montreal. Normally, a college basketball summer exhibition tour doesn't attract much attention. Elite American schools almost always blow out the weaker international teams. Typically, only a few hundred fans show up to games.

This was completely different.

All three games sold out. Crowds of 5,490 packed the gym in suburban Toronto for the first two games, and an incredible 10,098 came to watch in Montreal. The interest was so great that ESPN broadcast all three games in the United States and TSN, the sports network in Canada, did the same there. ESPN+ even did an all-access show with Coach K in preparation for the tour.

Call it the Zion factor. Suddenly, meaningless games against opponents almost no one had ever heard of were worthy of national attention. ESPN even sent its top broadcast crew—Dan Shulman and Jay Bilas—to call the action.

And there was plenty of action. The first game was against Ryerson University, and it didn't take long for Zion to get going. Just twenty-three seconds into the game, Zion caught an outlet pass at half-court and began charging to the net. He took two dribbles, leaped into the air, and scooped in a layup. At about 285 pounds, his ability to fly was astounding. He later got the crowd buzzing with blocked shots and strong rebounds, and even hit three of four from behind the three-point line.

Zion finished with 29 points and 13 rebounds. RJ poured in 34, and Duke won easily, 86–67, against an overmatched opponent. Zion was just excited to finally wear the Duke jersey.

"Putting those four letters across your chest," Zion said of the D-U-K-E on his uniform. "It's like a dream come true."

A few nights later, Zion scored 24 and Duke won again, 96–60, over the University of Toronto. Then, in Montreal, they beat McGill University 103–58, with Zion having 36 points, 13 rebounds, 4 assists, 3 steals, and 2 blocks. The game also included some absurd dunks that were splashed across social media and *SportsCenter*.

The Canadian teams weren't at anywhere near Duke's level, but there was no denying that Zion was something else. And the regular season hadn't even started yet.

"I thought he was going to be good," Coach K said, "but he's a really special player."

Soaring with confidence from the Canada trip, Duke took a break as the fall semester started and then got back to practice in October. By November, it was time for the regular season, where the competition promised to be far tougher.

Duke's season opener was in Indianapolis at what is called the Champions Classic. It's a doubleheader featuring four of the best programs in the country, and this year would be no different. Duke was ranked number 4 in the Associated Press poll of sportswriters. In the first round, it would play against number 2, Kentucky, while number 1, Kansas, would face off with 10th-ranked Michigan State.

It was an exciting way to kick off the season, and a big television audience tuned in to watch. The game was played at Bankers Life Fieldhouse in downtown Indianapolis, home of the NBA's Indiana Pacers. Because there were so many NBA prospects on the four teams, the stands weren't packed with just basketball fans, but also scouts and general managers, who would make draft selections the following June.

There was a lot on the line. Everyone had heard

(and even seen) how good the Duke freshmen were, especially Zion. But watching the prospects beat up on Canadian teams and viewing old high school highlights didn't count. The University of Kentucky was different.

In addition to its incredible championship legacy, Kentucky had the second-best recruiting class of the year, featuring future NBA players such as Tyler Herro and Keldon Johnson. Some good upperclassmen had also returned, and, as always, the team was considered a national title contender.

Heading into the season, Zion wasn't even considered the best Duke freshman. A lot of media had RJ pegged as the freshman and player of the year, not just in the Atlantic Coast Conference, but nationally. No one was doubting Zion, but his style of play was unique, so no one was quite sure what he would do. Now here was his chance to show them.

Zion admitted that he was nervous as the game approached. Coach K wasn't worried and decided to start four freshmen in the season opener—Zion, RJ, Cam, and Tre. Fortunately, they had upperclassmen on the bench, including Jack and Javin, to tell them to just relax and not sweat the pressure.

"You just learn from the upperclassmen," Zion

said. "If you go in too excited, things will not go your way. Just play very hard."

He and his teammates played not just hard, they played brilliantly. It was like they had been shot out of a cannon. A big bucket here, a defensive stop there, then a thundering rebound, then a three-pointer. It was complete domination. With millions of fans ready to see a hard-fought game, Duke jumped to a 10-point lead after six minutes and a 21-point lead after ten. Kentucky didn't stand a chance.

RJ scored 33. Zion had 28 points and hit 11 of 13 shots. He also grabbed 7 rebounds. Duke won 118–84.

"When you start four freshmen, no matter how talented they are, you don't know what they are going to do in this environment against an outstanding team," Coach K said. "They were magnificent tonight ... This was one of those nights where at the start we were doing everything. I mean, everything."

Duke now had America's attention. The highlights from the game were everywhere on traditional and social media. The pounding of Kentucky made everyone wonder if Duke should be the favorites to win the national title. Even though Duke was just

1–0 on the season, some people were already wondering if the Blue Devils could go undefeated.

This wasn't Coach K's first time leading a great team, so he was going to do everything he could to make sure they ignored the hype. "When you're playing in our program, you have to keep balanced," he said.

"We have noticed that we are getting a lot of attention," Zion said. "But people have to understand— it's one game. There's about thirty-nine, forty more games left. If you focus on one game in the past, it's not doing anything for you in the future."

In their next game, Duke defeated Army 94–72, but the game was close until the final ten minutes or so. Zion had 27 points and 16 rebounds, but he knew Army wasn't nearly as talented as the Blue Devils, or even Kentucky. They had simply outworked the Duke players at the start of the game.

That was another lesson Zion needed to learn. In high school ball, there might be a few big games, but then you might be able to coast for a week or two against weaker opponents. You can't do that in college, where the schedule never lets up. And you definitely can't do it in the NBA, where even the worst team in the league can win on a given night.

"It's one thing for somebody to tell you that everybody's going to bring their best against you, that all their shots are going to feel like they're going in," Williamson said. "But I think until you truly experience it, I think you just have to go through it to fully understand."

Unfazed by the expectations, Duke began to get serious. They crushed Eastern Michigan University 84–46 in their next game. During one stretch of the easy victory, Zion threw an alley-oop to RJ, who slammed it home. Then on the next possession, RJ threw a similar pass to Zion, who hammered it in. The Cameron Crazies couldn't scream loud enough, and all across America, Duke was becoming must-see TV, if only for Zion's dunks.

"More so than how high he jumps is his incredible body control, especially on a fast break," Coach K said. "Even though 'slither' isn't a word you would normally use to describe [how someone his size moves], he basically does that, which is crazy."

The Blue Devils weren't just the most exciting team in the country. The AP poll said they were the best, ranking them at number 1 nationally.

"It is great to be number 1, but nobody really

cares who's number 1 right now," Zion said. "The goal is to win a championship in March."

Up next, another prestigious event and an even better travel experience. Duke headed to Maui, Hawaii, to play in the Maui Invitational during Thanksgiving Week. Each year the Invitational hosts some of the best teams in the country. Players and coaches love it because when they aren't playing or practicing, there are a beach, a pool, and the tropical weather to enjoy.

This was a business trip, though, not a vacation, Coach K reminded the team. The field included number 8, Auburn, and number 3, Gonzaga, both very talented teams. But Duke, with its number-1 ranking and a roster filled with NBA-bound star freshmen, was the clear target. Every player in Maui knew this was an opportunity to prove himself.

In the Maui Invitational opener, Duke had no problem beating San Diego State, 90–64. Zion, however, was in foul trouble for much of the game and played for just eighteen minutes. The Blue Devils didn't need him this time, but it was clear that avoiding fouls was something he had to work on.

The next day's opponent was a more difficult

challenge—a very good Auburn team that would reach the Final Four of March Madness later that season. The game was hard fought, and early on Coach K saw something new out of Zion—some nerves. Maybe it was the quality of the opponent. Maybe it was the struggles of the game the day before. Whatever it was, Zion wasn't himself. If nothing else, he wasn't wearing that big grin out on the court.

"He usually is a kid that's having a lot of fun," Coach K said.

During a first-half timeout, Coach K spoke directly to Zion. "Smile," the coach said. "Have fun."

Just like that, Zion relaxed. Duke took a big lead and then held off a late Auburn rally to win, 78–72. Zion had 13 points and 9 rebounds—not big numbers by his standards, but he hit a critical basket late to ice the game.

"I thought that was the play of the game," Coach K said.

Next up, the championship game against 3rd-ranked Gonzaga University. Gonzaga is a small private school in Spokane, Washington, but it has a great basketball tradition and is often a national title contender. This year was no different, and its game against the Blue Devils was one of the best of the season.

With a huge audience watching at home, the two teams played at a very high level. Gonzaga took a 17-point lead in the second half, but Duke kept clawing back. RJ scored 23. Zion had 22. But after cutting the Gonzaga lead to just 2 points, they couldn't score on the final possession.

Duke lost. They were now 5–1 on the season. The thing was, Coach K wasn't even that upset. "Good game," he called it. While the players were disappointed, the veteran coach saw a young team, starting four freshmen, that had played a tough early-season schedule and performed well. If anything, it was good to end all the "undefeated" talk. Coach K said he loved how quickly this collection of individuals had become a team.

"They're over themselves," Coach K said. "It's not about them. They're very secure and they have been parented well, they have been coached well, and so they understand being part of something bigger than them . . . We learned a lot here."

The learning experience—and the wins that would come as a result—was just getting started.

SA 106 | NO 104

SA 106 | NO 107

"Zion four for four from three!!!"

9

The Sneaker

AT THAT POINT in the college basketball season, it was all Zion, all the time. Following the Maui Invitational, Duke rolled through most of its competition, with its superstar freshmen leading the way. Each contest felt more like a parade of alley-oops and windmill dunks than an actual game. It was usually Zion and RJ just trying to one-up each other.

The games were often massacres. They beat Hartford by 30, Yale by 33, Princeton by 51, and Stetson by 64 points—113–49. Even bigger, more talented programs that should have been able to put up a fight didn't fare much better. Duke hammered Indiana by 21, Notre Dame by 22, Boston College by 25, and St. John's by 30.

Zion got a chance to play Clemson, and he showed them what they'd missed out on not just by scoring 25 points, but also by throwing down a 360-degree dunk—he leaped and spun a full rotation in the air before slamming the ball through the hoop.

"I looked back to see if anybody was there," Zion said. "Nobody was. And it was just poetry in motion. Float in the air and at the last second you just punch it and the crowd just goes into a frenzy. I love it."

It seemed that almost no one knew how to stop the Blue Devils. Generally, opposing coaches left the game grumbling about what had just happened to them.

"I've never faced a team like that," the Stetson coach said.

"Talented, unselfish," the St. John's coach said.

"They're really gifted," the Notre Dame coach said.

Duke wasn't perfect. There were a number of close games. And the Blue Devils even lost to Syracuse in overtime, despite a 35-point performance from Zion. For the most part though, the team looked every bit as good as its members dreamed it might be.

That included Zion, of course. As the season went on, it was clear that he wasn't just an incredible player, but a player unlike any that anyone had ever seen. His size. His strength. His agility. That much was obvious with each steal or dunk.

It was the other things, though. The passing. The rebounding. The effort.

And it was the way he played with joy and happiness and how he rarely, if ever, protested a foul against him. Avoiding foul trouble was the one part of Zion's game that he struggled with. Maybe it was because of his size, but he tended to pick up cheap fouls and occasionally find himself on the bench so he wouldn't foul out. Yet even then he tried to help the team. Rather than pout or complain, he would support his teammates, especially by rooting on Jack White, who usually subbed in for him.

"[Foul trouble] is very frustrating but I think it would be very selfish of me to be in my own head," Zion said. "I just need to cheer for my teammates."

Zion was a star who acted like a guy fighting for every second of playing time.

"He just plays so dang hard," Boston College coach Jim Christian said after Zion manhandled his team to the tune of 16 points, 17 rebounds, 4 steals, and 3 blocks. "His second effort to get balls is unlike anybody I've ever seen . . . To me, that's a straight winner, that's what it is. That's a straight winner."

With each dominating performance, Zion's fame grew. He quickly found that he couldn't lead a normal life. He was still just a college kid, but almost everywhere he went, people were asking for selfies or autographs. And at his size, there was no way to hide.

"Going to the gas station, I go in there [and] I'm going to at least be in there 10 minutes because somebody wants to have a conversation," Zion said. "I mean, I can't even go to the bathroom sometimes without people bothering me.

"But yeah, I did take a look at myself in the mirror and said, 'This is the life I wanted to be a part of,'" Zion continued. "My parents told me all this would happen, so it's not much of a shock, but when it happens you're like, you've got to take a step back and you go, wow—I guess I'm on it."

Zion tried to do his best to avoid being bigger than the team. He wanted people talking about Duke, not him. It wasn't easy, though. After practice one day during the summer trip in Canada, the players were having fun trying out different dunks. At one point RJ ran down the court and took off from behind the foul line, which is fifteen feet from the basket, flew in, and dunked it. Everyone went wild.

Zion decided he'd try it, also. That's a long way for a man his size to soar, but he came sprinting to the line, took off, and slammed the ball in. There were a lot of people videotaping the dunk and a clip was soon posted on social media and went viral. It even started showing up on television highlight shows. So there was all this attention on his big dunk, but not on RJ's. Zion could see the problem. Social media could be fun, but it could also be a poison.

"RJ literally took off from the free-throw line like two seconds before me, but people weren't giving him credit for that," Zion said. "And I don't want to be the guy to take away light from other players. That's why I really haven't done it since. I said when people started giving my teammates the respect that they deserve, then I guess I'll start doing more stuff like that. But it hasn't really changed."

Across the 2018–19 season, Duke was the nation's most popular team. On ESPN, college basketball games drew an average of 1.2 million viewers. For Duke broadcasts, it was 2.14 million. So almost a million more people tuned in when Duke was playing than for a typical college basketball game. Simply put, everyone wanted to see what Zion would do next.

It wasn't just on television, either. Every Duke game, home and away, was sold out. Among the crowd were plenty of celebrities. Boxer Floyd Mayweather came to a game at Cameron. So did former NBA great Dwyane Wade, filmmaker Spike Lee, and actresses such as Peyton List and Hayden Panettiere.

When Duke visited the University of Pittsburgh, rapper/businessman Jay-Z sat in the front row. Zion dropped 25 points for him en route to another big victory.

"When he walks in, with his squad, you look over and you're like, 'Oh, my God, that's him,'" Zion said. "That was like a dream come true."

When Duke played at Virginia, LeBron James showed up. LeBron and the Los Angeles Lakers were scheduled to play in Philadelphia the next night. With a day off, LeBron rented a jet and took a short flight to Charlottesville, Virginia.

LeBron has always liked watching young stars and

dropping in on college games. Plus, he had played in two Olympics for Coach K, so he liked to check in on him, as well. The Zion Experience was a little different from a normal college game, though, since the level of hype was similar to what LeBron had experienced as a high school senior.

"I can relate in a sense of he's been covered [in the media] since he was in high school and everybody is trying to compare him to the 'next this' or the 'next that,'" LeBron said. "But the best thing I've noticed is he seems like a good kid. He seems like he's got his head on straight . . . Everybody gets so caught up in the game itself. I look at the intangibles and he seems like he has great intangibles and seems like a great kid."

But there was no bigger name to come to a game than President Barack Obama himself, a longtime basketball fan. And there was certainly no bigger game for him to attend than that late February clash with Carolina at Cameron.

Not long after Zion received recruiting letters from Duke and UNC, in which each school expressed its hope that he would come play for it, Zion Williamson had begun thinking about what it might be like to play in a Blue Devils–Tar Heels game.

Every year the two schools, separated by just 9.8 miles, meet at least twice, for one home game each. Both games are highly anticipated, both schools usually field top teams, and include some of the greatest players and most exciting finishes in basketball history.

While Zion had spent much of his recruitment believing he'd play in his home state at either Clemson or South Carolina, the appeal of being a part of the Duke–Carolina rivalry was always in the back of his mind. There's nothing else like it in college basketball.

And now it was here. The date was February 20, 2019. Duke was 23–2 and ranked number 1 in the country. UNC was 20–5 and ranked 8th. The game was beyond hyped. Fans and the media had been discussing it for months. Cameron Indoor Stadium was sold out, of course, although you could still buy a seat on the secondary ticket market . . . if you were rich. The cheapest one was about $2,900 just before tip-off. One person paid $10,652 online for a single ticket.

Whoever managed to snag a seat would be joined by no less than former president Obama, who flew in to watch the game from the front row. This is the kind of electric atmosphere that you can't get at most schools. It's part of why Zion had chosen Duke. Of course, he also could have chosen UNC and been playing for the other side.

"We tried to recruit him very, very hard," UNC coach Roy Williams said.

Now Coach Williams was dealing with the ultimate basketball nightmare, watching Zion suit up for his archrival as the whole country, and its former president, watched.

"Name somebody else that's got the skill set that he has," Coach Williams said. "Because in the college game, I've never seen it. Everybody will say, 'Well, what about LeBron?' Listen to what I said. LeBron never played in college. I've never seen anything like [Zion]."

As the game tipped off, the atmosphere inside the building was electric.

UNC scored first to take a 2–0 lead. Then just thirty-six seconds into the game, Zion dribbled across the top of the key, planted his left foot down, and began to spin back to his right and away from his defender. Yet while his sneaker planted on the hardwood, his foot didn't. Zion was applying so much weight with so much force that the shoe split apart at the seam. His foot blasted through the sneaker, ripping a huge hole in it. It caused him to fall to the floor and lose the ball.

All over Cameron, let alone at home on television, it was a challenge to figure out what had happened. No one had ever seen such a thing before.

"His shoe broke," President Obama, sitting courtside, said while pointing at what was left of the Nike.

It was wild. Yet no one was laughing because Zion remained down on the court, grabbing his right knee. The busted shoe had caused him to sort of do a split, straining his right knee. He was clearly in pain. Cameron Indoor, known as the loudest gym in basketball and just a moment prior all worked up for the UNC game, fell into silence and worry.

Was it serious? Was it something that could threaten Zion's career, just as he was on the cusp of NBA millions? Was this the last Duke fans would see of this big-smiling, high-flying star?

Slowly, Zion was taken to the Duke locker room. He didn't return that night, as his shell-shocked Blue Devil teammates, minus the squad's star, got blown out, 88–72.

Zion was hurt. The question was, how badly?

10

The Decision

Zion was diagnosed with a "grade-one right knee sprain." While any injury is cause for concern, grade one is considered mild, and Zion and his fans immediately breathed sighs of relief. Duke listed him as "day-to-day," which meant he might return to action at any point. The question was whether he *should* return.

Zion had proved himself to be the best player in college basketball, even better than RJ, who was having an incredible season himself. Zion was unique, the kind of talent that didn't come along very often.

If he chose to go pro after just one college season, whatever NBA team was given the number-1 pick in the upcoming draft would be almost sure to select him. There was nothing left for him to do in the NCAA, some argued.

Then there was his popularity—and his marketability. With the big television ratings he drew and his enormous social media following, Zion was in line to receive offers from companies, especially sneaker companies, willing to pay him tens of millions of dollars to endorse their products once he went pro.

NCAA rules didn't allow Zion to get paid while playing at Duke. He received a good deal as part of his athletic scholarship—free tuition and room and board and a small monthly stipend (plus health care and expert coaching). But it didn't compare to the millions and millions he would make once he went to the NBA. At this point, the only thing standing between Zion and the kind of money that would set him and his family up for life was . . . injury.

For Nike, which had manufactured the sneakers worn by Duke's players, the failure of its shoe was an incredible embarrassment. Millions of people were watching live, and tens of millions would see replays on social media. To make matters worse, the injury occurred not in the flow of regular basketball action, but during a routine moment. That can happen. In this case, it was the fault of the Paul George 2.5 shoes on Zion's size-15 feet. If the sole of the shoe hadn't broken, he would've been fine.

"We are obviously concerned and want to wish Zion a speedy recovery," Nike said in a statement.

Nike was so concerned that the morning after the Duke–UNC game, it flew a team of experts and shoe designers from its headquarters outside Portland, Oregon, to Durham to inspect the shoe. It then sent the same team to its factory in China, where it helped create a fortified sneaker that it believed could withstand anything even Zion could hit it with. They also told Zion to replace each pair of shoes after just a few games "because of the wear and tear," Coach K said. "I think that contributed to the blowout."

Zion missed the next five games, including losses to Virginia Tech and again to North Carolina. With each game missed, more and more people were debating whether Zion should just relax until he could cash in on an NBA contract and endorsement deals rather than risk another injury.

"Zion needs to chill out the rest of the season," Atlanta Hawks star Trae Young tweeted.

"I think he's locked up the biggest shoe deal," said former great Scottie Pippen, who won six NBA championships with the Chicago Bulls. "I think he's definitely going to be the number 1 pick. I think he's done enough for college basketball that it's more about him personally now. I think for him as a young player that I would shut it down."

Zion saw it differently. If his main concern had been avoiding injury until he made the NBA, then he would have skipped college altogether and spent the year training. He almost certainly would have been a top-5 pick even if he hadn't played at Duke. Plus, he noted, you can get injured just practicing.

He had chosen to play college basketball and chosen to play specifically at Duke for a reason. He loved it. He loved the competition and his teammates and the coaching. He had made a commitment and he wasn't going to skip out on it. Part of the Duke appeal was the Brotherhood. Well, he said, you can't bail on your brothers.

"I can't just stop playing," Zion said. "I'd be letting my teammates down. I'd be letting Coach K down. I'd be letting a lot of people down. If I wanted to sit out, I wouldn't have gone to college. I came to Duke to play."

It took three weeks of rest and rehab before Zion was allowed to return to the court. Duke wanted to be cautious, both for the long-term health of Zion and to make sure he was ready for the postseason. No matter how many times Zion asked to get back into uniform before he was cleared to play, the doctors stuck to the plan.

Zion returned in time for the Atlantic Coast Conference Tournament, which was held in Charlotte, North Carolina. For Duke to win the event, it would need to play on three consecutive nights. It would be a big test for Zion and Duke. Could Zion's knee handle that? Should he risk it? Was he even going to be the same player when he returned, or would he play cautiously to avoid another injury?

The answer came about two minutes in, when Zion stole the ball in a pass by a Syracuse player, dribbled down the court, and leaped through the air before powering home a huge slam dunk. It was the first of five dunks that night as Zion hit all 13 of his shots and finished with 29 points to lead Duke to the 84–72 victory.

Just like that, Zion was back.

Up next was North Carolina, which pleased Zion. He had been looking forward to being a part of the Blue Devils–Tar Heels rivalry, but he'd lasted just thirty-six seconds of the first game, and then missed the second. Now, in the ACC Tournament, he'd get his chance.

Carolina was a great team also, though, and when they took a 13-point first-half lead, it looked like they might cruise to another victory. That's when Zion got going. He drained a three-pointer. He crushed home a dunk. He snagged a rebound in traffic. He finished an alley-oop, then a steal and another dunk. Duke chipped into the lead until it made a full comeback. During the entire second half, the scoreboard kept going back and forth, with each team constantly trading off the lead.

Finally, with about thirty seconds remaining, UNC led 73–72. With a chance to be a hero, Zion got the ball on the left side, spun his way into the lane, and put up a shot about six feet from the basket. With millions of fans looking on . . . it missed, bouncing off the rim.

However, Zion wasn't ready to accept a loss. He was so quick and so good at anticipating where the ball was headed that he sprang back up to the rim between three UNC players and grabbed his own rebound. He then tipped it back up and in!

Seconds later, UNC missed a final shot and Duke won, 74–73. Zion had 31 points and 11 rebounds—including the game-winning final bucket.

His impact on the Duke–Carolina rivalry was secured.

"The guy that's been hurt came back and put on his Superman jersey," UNC coach Roy Williams said. "[Zion] was incredible. It's such a blend of strength and power and quickness that we couldn't stop him from getting the basketball inside and going to the basket."

The next day Duke beat Florida State, 73–63, to win the ACC Championship. Zion led the Blue Devils in scoring again, with 21 points. He was named the tournament's most outstanding player. His Nikes didn't break. He said his knee felt fine.

Not a bad return for a guy who many had assumed was done for the year.

After winning the trophy, Zion and his teammates climbed a ladder to clip down the nets at the ACC Tournament, a symbol to everyone who'd said he should just rest up for the NBA.

"I made a commitment to [my teammates]," Zion

said. "I would be a bad person if I went back on my commitment . . . When you're a little kid watching Duke on TV cut down nets, championship nets, and you say you want to be a part of it, you say it as a little kid. But when you actually grow up and get to be a part of it, [it's awesome]."

Duke was now 29–5 and was given a number-1 seed in the NCAA Tournament. It would need to win six games to capture the national championship, but it had its star big man back.

The Blue Devils would be the favorites to win it all.

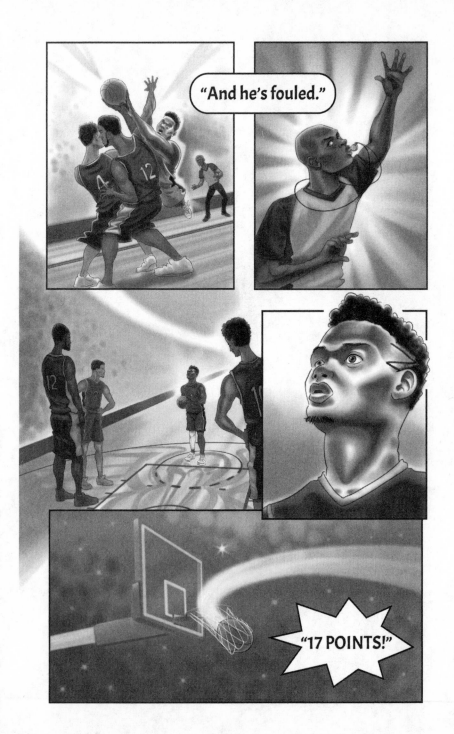

11

NCAA Tournament

EVERY COLLEGE BASKETBALL PLAYER wants to compete in the NCAA Tournament. The big crowds. The excitement. The competition. The one-and-done nature of the event—lose and your season is over. It feels like all of America is watching, even people who don't normally follow college basketball.

For Zion, the first two rounds of the tournament brought added anticipation: They were going to be played at Colonial Life Arena in Columbia, South Carolina. It is normally the home court of the University of South Carolina. But now it represented an unexpected chance for Zion to play college basketball in his home state.

"Once I committed to Duke . . . I didn't think I would ever have a chance to play in the state of South Carolina in a college basketball game," Zion said. "So I'm very excited about that. [However] I can't put my personal excitement ahead of my teammates because, at the end of the day, I'm on a team. And I want to win with my teammates."

Now here he was, back home. The first-round opponent was North Dakota State University (NDSU), a team the Blue Devils were expected to wallop. Instead they led just 31–27 at halftime. That's when Zion took over. He slammed home a rebound off a missed free throw. Minutes later he stole the ball, went behind his back to lose a defender, and scooped in a layup. He finished with 25 points and Duke cruised to an 85–62 victory.

During the NDSU game, the CBS crew broadcasting the game used something the network called the "Zion Cam," basically a camera that was focused solely on Zion and followed him everywhere he went. That's how big a star he had become. He had his own camera. Zion did his best to ignore it.

"I was just focused on trying to go out there and help my team win," he said.

That was Zion. The bigger the spotlight, the more attention and awards he won, the more he tried to refocus on team play. He was the star, but he didn't want to be the star.

"None of that fazes him," Coach K said. "He's all about his team, really, and about winning. It's amazing, when people who are really good don't seek attention, they get more. It's the people who don't necessarily have the ability, they seek attention, and then they get pressured and all that. He doesn't seek attention. He seeks winning and playing really well. He sees pure. He's pure, bottom line . . . He's got it all and [was] brought up the right way. He's got great parents and [a great] value system, everything. It's remarkable, really."

In the second round, Zion would face his biggest challenge—or at least his tallest. The opponent was the University of Central Florida (UCF). Their best player was a center from Senegal named Tacko Fall, who stood seven-foot-five, a full eleven inches taller than Zion.

Tacko is so tall, and his arms are so long, that he

can dunk a basketball without even jumping! He just needs to get up on his toes, reach up, and lay the ball over the rim. He hit 74 percent of his shots—most of them dunks—during the season, the highest shooting percentage in the history of college basketball. Defensively he is a menace. He averaged 2.6 blocks a game that year and would have had more if he hadn't scared so many opponents away from even attempting a shot.

Tacko knew how big the challenge was going to be trying to stop Zion. He was confident, though, and even vowed to stop Zion from dunking on him for the entire game. "It's very hard [to dunk on me]," Tacko told NCAA.com. "I won't allow it. I won't allow him [to put] me on one of his highlight tapes."

When the media presented that quote to Zion, he could only shrug. He liked playing confident opponents and, of course, trying to dunk on a seven-foot-five player would be tough.

"What is he supposed to say?" Zion said. "Is he supposed to say I'm going to dunk on him? He said the right thing, but I'm not really focused on that. I'm just focused on trying to help my team win the game. Nobody's going to be intimidated on the court."

Tacko turned out to be a real challenge for Zion. UCF had a terrific team and the game was one of the hardest of the season for Duke. Every time it started to look like Duke would pull away, UCF surged back. As Tacko predicted, Zion couldn't figure out how to dunk over him and had to stay, at least partially, on the outside and shoot three-pointers. Meanwhile, Tacko had 7 dunks.

A key point in the game was when Tacko was whistled for his fourth foul, meaning just one more and he'd be out of the game. He had to go sit on the bench. That's when Zion was able to take over. He would score 32 points in the game. Yet once Tacko got back in there, here came UCF again.

With 2:09 remaining in the game, Tacko slammed home another dunk to give UCF a 74–70 lead. Duke's season was suddenly on the brink. One loss and they were out of the tournament. During a stoppage in play, Coach K gathered the team and looked right at his freshmen, especially Zion and RJ.

"You guys live for these moments," Coach K said.

Zion nodded. "I consider him the greatest coach of all time," he said. "When he looks at you and tells you that . . . It's like the most confidence you can be given."

Cam Reddish hit a three for Duke to cut the lead to 74–73. Then UCF hit two free throws to push the lead back to 76–73. With eighteen seconds left, Zion got the ball on the left wing. He knew he had to do something. It was now or never. He had one man guarding him while Tacko stood underneath the basket, ready to block anything he could.

This was no time to be afraid of this seven-foot-five giant. Zion drove to the center of the lane, then pivoted and quickly spun back, losing his defender. It was now just him and Tacko, and Zion couldn't back down. He took one step toward the basket and leaped directly into Tacko, who had his hands high in the air. As they collided, Zion somehow got a shot off. The ball hit the front of the rim, lay there for a moment, and fell in, right as the referee called a foul on Tacko.

Just like that, Duke was within one, Zion was on the foul line with a chance to tie the game, and Tacko had fouled out.

"You know, it's March Madness," Zion said later. "I went to the basket."

Zion never did dunk on Tacko, but he did score the most important basket of the game. Down one, Zion still had to make the free throw to tie. If there was one weak part of his game, this was it. Despite working on it all year, he was only a 64 percent free-throw shooter. He had hit five of six free throws against UCF, though.

With the game and the season at stake, he stepped up to the foul line, went through his routine, shot . . . and missed.

With Tacko fouled out, however, UCF couldn't grab the rebound. Instead, RJ crashed the boards, snatched the ball, and laid up a short shot to give Duke the lead, 77–76.

UCF then barely missed a running jumper and a put back—both shots rolled off the rim—and the time ran out as the Blue Devils raced to celebrate.

Duke had survived.

"The will to win of Zion and RJ," Coach K said, "you can't measure it. We haven't had a team play any better against us than [UCF] did."

The victory pushed Duke into the "Sweet Sixteen"—meaning that they were one of the sixteen teams still in the tournament. They next met Virginia Tech, who, much like UCF, played a very strong game, even leading at the half. In the end, Zion scored 23 points and RJ had 18 and dished 11 assists. Virginia Tech had a last-second shot roll off the rim (very similar to the UCF game) and Duke pushed through 75–73.

Now only Michigan State stood between the Blue Devils and the Final Four. However, there was plenty of reason for concern. Duke had won all three of its games thus far in the tournament, but it hadn't looked dominant in any of them. Both the UCF and Virginia Tech games had been closer than expected. How many times could the Blue Devils survive at the buzzer? Plus, Cam Reddish, one of the key freshmen, had missed the last game with a knee injury.

Standing in their way was a talented Michigan State team filled with veterans. They had a star point guard, Cassius Winston, and a bunch of big, strong front-court players who had their own Final Four and national championship dreams. The Spartans weren't going to be intimidated by Zion and the Blue Devils.

"That's why you come to college," Zion said. "To be a part of games like this."

The game was a classic, a heavyweight bout between two of the great programs in college basketball. All season Zion had been the deciding factor in games due to his combination of size, strength, and power. MSU's star, Cassius Winston, however, stood just six foot one and wasn't even particularly fast. That's one of the best things about basketball. The top player isn't always the biggest and strongest player. Cassius threw alley-oop passes to his teammates. Zion caught them from his teammates.

Cassius would score 20 points and record 10 assists, and MSU got a critical three-pointer with 34.3 seconds left, giving that team a 68–66 lead. Duke had another chance, though. With 5.2 seconds left, RJ drove to the basket and was fouled. He just needed to hit two free throws to tie the game and maybe force overtime.

But he missed the first. Just like that, Duke was in trouble. Coach K called a play where RJ would try to miss the second free throw in the hope that Zion, or any Blue Devil, could snare the rebound and score. Instead, RJ's attempted miss bounced high off the back of the rim only to fall back through the basket.

Duke couldn't catch a break. They were now down one, but Michigan State had the chance to inbound the ball and run out the clock. They got it to Cassius, who raced around the court and wasted away the remaining 5.2 seconds. In an instant, Duke's season was done and Zion's national title hopes were crushed. Michigan State advanced to the Final Four courtesy of a 68–67 victory.

A stunned Zion tried to console his devastated teammates as they walked off the court. In his final Duke game, he had had 24 points and 14 rebounds, but it hadn't been enough.

"I'm very upset, obviously, because we wanted to go to the Final Four," Zion said. "But congrats to Michigan State. They deserve it . . . They're a great team. They played a great game. And [Cassius] Winston, he took over."

Zion returned to Durham and tried to enjoy his final few weeks as a college student. The loss hung over him, but other than winning a national championship, he had gotten nearly everything he ever could have hoped for in playing for Duke. Great coaching, lifelong friends, and a spot in the Brotherhood.

He was named the National Player of the Year in college basketball, but when accepting the trophy, he spent most of the time deflecting the praise.

"I see it as a team award because without my teammates, I wouldn't be here," Zion said.

The Duke experience had been great, but now it was time for the next step—the NBA draft.

12

New Orleans

FULTON STREET SQUARE is an outdoor shopping and dining area in the Warehouse District of New Orleans. On June 20, 2019, it was party central for the NBA.

That night, the league's annual draft was set to be held in New York City. The New Orleans Pelicans owned the number-1 overall selection. There was no doubt they were going to select Zion Williamson.

When the Pelicans won the league's draft lottery and the right to pick whomever they wanted from the ranks of college basketball, the employees of their ticket sales department, watching on television, erupted into a frenzy. They knew that if Zion was coming, their jobs selling tickets to games were about to get easy. Indeed, the office phone started ringing immediately.

Now here was the proof. The excitement in New Orleans was so great, the team decided to create a central spot for fans to celebrate and watch the draft on big outdoor televisions. A brass band played. The Pelicans' dance team performed. A drum line entertained. Free T-shirts were handed out. It was a great night for Pelican fans.

And when the announcement finally came and Zion, wearing an all-white suit, rose to shake the hand of NBA commissioner Adam Silver, the cheers and screams could be heard all over the city.

Zion, however, was quiet and overwhelmed with emotion. He'd been dreaming of this for so long, he said it hardly felt real.

"I mean, I don't know what to say. I didn't think I'd be in this position," Zion said on the ESPN broadcast. Then he began to choke up and cry. "My mom sacrificed a lot for me. I wouldn't be here without my mom. She did everything for me. I just want to thank her . . . She put her dreams aside for mine.

She always looked out for the family first before herself."

Zion's mom was standing beside him and gave him a hug.

"To watch his hard work pay off, to watch this, we are just so happy for him," she said.

Finally, Zion was asked what he wanted to tell all those fans back in New Orleans, including the ones partying at Fulton Street. His eyes brightened and he broke into a smile.

"Let's dance," he said. "Let's dance."

The Pelicans certainly needed the boost of confidence. The team had been in existence since 2002, but had never advanced past the Western Conference Semifinals. It was coming off a 33–49 season. It had recently traded its star player, center Anthony Davis, to the Los Angeles Lakers, in part because Davis didn't believe the team was going to be a title contender anytime soon.

This was a new day, though. In the trade with the Lakers, New Orleans had gotten a bunch of future draft picks and some excellent young players, including talented point guard Lonzo Ball and high-scoring wingman Brandon Ingram. And now they had Zion.

When he arrived in town the day after the draft,

he was greeted by billboards welcoming him and by a lot of media, including twenty television cameras, just to film him walking into the Pelicans' practice facility. New Orleans wanted this to feel like more than just a new job. They wanted it to feel like family, sort of like the Brotherhood of Duke that Zion cherished.

Zion "is all about others, all about team, all about family, and not about himself," said David Griffin, the team's executive vice president. "The reason that was so meaningful for us is that's all we want to build. Everything we do is about adding members to this family that reflect the same values Zion's family has instilled him."

Zion was still just nineteen years old. Most people that age are either attending college or still living with their parents. Now he was a professional. And a well-paid one. He would earn about $10 million per season through his NBA salary. He also signed a $75 million endorsement deal with Nike (only LeBron James had gotten more as a rookie). And he inked deals with, among others, NBA 2K, Gatorade, and Mountain Dew, which included PepsiCo, the soft drink's maker, refurbishing an outdoor basketball court back in Spartanburg.

Zion was now a very wealthy young man.

That was nice, but that wasn't what motivated him. Winning did. Being there for his teammates did. Building a foundation that could lead to a championship one day did.

It's why, as detailed in the opening chapter, he was willing to be patient to return following the knee surgery that left him sidelined for the first few months of the season. Although he was dying to get back out on the court, there was no sense in taking on added risk with his knee. His health was too important.

But eventually, his recovery progressed and he got back in on the action. Two days after his debut against the Spurs, Zion played nearly 21 minutes and scored 15 points in a loss to Denver. He then played 27 minutes in a victory over Boston, nearly 30 while helping to defeat Cleveland, and just shy of 29 in a win against Memphis, where he ran into his old AAU teammate Ja Morant.

It wasn't just Zion who had soared into the NBA. Ja had, as well. When bigger schools ignored him in the recruitment process, Ja used that as motivation and became a star at Murray State in Kentucky. He wound up being the number-2 pick in the NBA

Draft, just behind his old AAU teammate. RJ Barrett went third, so Zion was surrounded by friends on draft night.

Now here was a game out of Zion and Ja's wildest dreams from their AAU days. Back then they were just two kids with potential but little hype. Now they were the future of the league, and they showed it. Zion had 24 points to Ja's 16. The Pelicans won, but afterward the two old friends hugged, traded jerseys, and talked about how far they had come.

"He knows he's my brother," Zion said of Ja. "[But] we are going to be rivals. That's just the South Carolina nature: to be dogs and go after each other. Off the court we know it's all love. But on the court, we're trying to win."

Zion was continuing to show why the Pelicans had decided to design their future around him as the centerpiece. NBA fans everywhere looked on with excitement. New Orleans, which in years past had rarely appeared on national television, were now regularly covered on ESPN and TNT. It was just like at Duke, and Zion, even playing limited minutes, didn't disappoint.

Ferocious dunks. Deep threes. That explosive first step that can take a breath away. He was everything everyone had hoped for. After eight games, he sat one out to rest his knee, but he soon returned.

He was even installed in the "Rising Stars" game during NBA All-Star weekend. One of his teammates? Ja, who during the game got loose on a fast break and threw a between-the-legs alley-oop to Zion, who pounded it down.

"After I caught it," Zion said with a laugh, "I was thinking about our Hornets days. And I keep thinking never in a million years would I have thought we'd have been in this game or been in the situation we're in."

In that same game Zion slammed home a two-handed dunk that was so powerful, it bent the backboard. A couple of stadium workers had to come out and fix it.

It was fun. The NBA was different from college, though. It was also a business. Zion was incredibly strong, but he was now playing against grown men who were fighting for their future, too. And it was a battle every night. Every player in the league is good. There were no easy matchups.

Plus, there were so many games in the season that being rested and ready was a major priority for Zion. In college you might play twice in a week and the games are forty minutes long. In the NBA, teams play four nights a week and the games stretch to forty-eight minutes. When games and practices are over, you don't just go back to the dorms with your buddies.

"On the court, I think it's the age difference," Zion said. "I'm 19, and you have some players in their 30s. Then off the court, just managing your time because in college you had practice but you also had class. In the NBA, it's practice and whatever you do with the rest of your day, you have to make the most of it."

Zion's playing time increased as the season went on. In his final eight games, he played at least thirty minutes a night—ideally, the plan was that over time, he'd build back up his strength and get to nearly forty per game. His scoring improved as well, including a 35-point performance against LeBron James and the Los Angeles Lakers.

That was a memorable night for Zion, who had grown up watching and dreaming of playing against LeBron. Now here they were, going back and forth, alley-oops, dunks, and steals. This time, the old legend won. LeBron had 40 and the Lakers took the victory. Zion, however, had held his own and sent a message that his time was coming.

"The kid's special, we all know that," LeBron said. "In today's game, where it's a track race, it's a fast pace, it's high tempo, it fits his game perfectly. They've got a good one . . . And every game is going to be another opportunity for him to get better."

It should have been. Unfortunately, Zion's rookie season was stopped just as he was heating up. The deadly and highly contagious coronavirus broke out worldwide, and in March of 2020 the NBA suspended play. Zion appeared in just nineteen games before the pandemic hit, averaging 23.6 points and 6.8 rebounds a game.

The NBA eventually returned in the summer of 2020. The league brought the top twenty-two teams to Orlando, Florida, where the players and coaches would stay in hotels on the campus of Disney World. The games would be played at the ESPN Wide World of Sports complex, which is part of Disney World. The complex is home to numerous youth sports tournaments and has baseball and softball diamonds, soccer and lacrosse fields, and a couple of small stadiums for basketball, gymnastics, and cheerleading competitions. Now it was home to the NBA.

New Orleans qualified to compete and Zion and his teammates moved into Disney World's Yacht Club Resort. They had nice rooms, restaurants, and all sorts of non-basketball entertainment, including fishing, Ping-Pong, and video games. The downside was that to stay safe from the coronavirus, they couldn't leave the area around their hotel or the arenas (called "the bubble"). That meant the rides of Disney World were close by, but off-limits.

Zion was there for business anyway. He had spent his time during the shutdown of the season working out with his stepfather. He had lost a few pounds and gotten into great shape. The goal was to make the most of the return to play and lead the Pelicans into the playoffs. It didn't work out so well.

The Pelicans continued to limit Zion's playing time—they wanted to hold him to about fifteen minutes a game to start so his knee wouldn't get injured. That not only upset his ability to get back into the flow of basketball, but the team's chance of winning games. In the end, New Orleans went just 2–6 and Zion played in just five of the games. He averaged 24.0 points a game in his final three appearances, but the Pelicans missed the playoffs and Coach Gentry was soon fired as coach.

This wasn't how Zion had envisioned his rookie year—the start delayed by injury, the conclusion suspended due to a virus before the team failed to reach the playoffs. His impact on the game of basketball was undeniable, though. So was his potential. There was little doubt that there would be many more incredible performances to come from the kid from South Carolina.

Instant Replay

The 4th quarter of Zion Williamson's NBA debut...

 SA 99   NO 91

"Zion stepping back..."

"... and hitting a three!"

 NO 94

SA 101 — NO 94

"Here's a lob to Zion..."

SA 106 NO 104

SA 106 NO 107

"Zion four for four from three!!!"

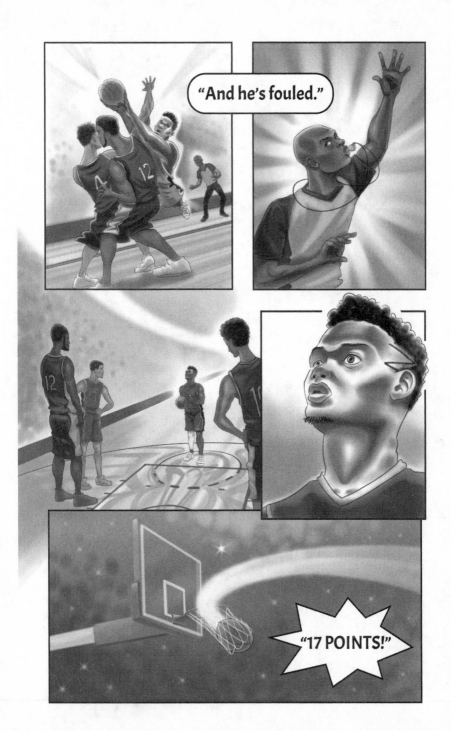

Hungry for More EPIC ATHLETES?
Look Out for These Superstar
Biographies, in Stores Now!

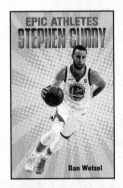

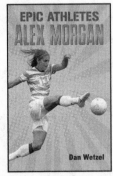

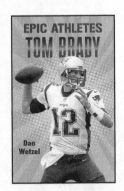

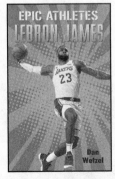

The Nonstop Sports Action Continues!

Here's an excerpt of
EPIC ATHLETES
KEVIN DURANT

Illustrated by Marcelo Baez

1

The Shot

IT WAS THE FINAL MINUTE of the fourth quarter
of Game 3 of the 2017 National Basketball Association (NBA) Finals and a single basket—or rebound,
steal, missed shot, or turnover—by either team
could swing not just this neck-and-neck contest, but
potentially the entire championship. The Cleveland
Cavaliers led the Golden State Warriors, 113–111
in a matchup that was about as close and tense as
basketball can get.

Golden State had jumped to a 2–0 lead in the
best-of-seven Finals, but heading into this contest,

the Warriors knew better than to get overconfident. Just a year prior they'd won seventy-three regular season games and led these same Cavs 3–1 in The Finals. They'd looked like one of the greatest teams in NBA history. Then LeBron James led a historic comeback that saw Cleveland win Games 5, 6, and 7 and take the NBA championship.

Now a year later, late in Game 3, every single Warriors player, coach, and fan had to wonder if LeBron might do enough to win this game and steal another championship from Golden State.

That's when Kevin Durant reached up high with his long, long right arm and snatched a missed Cleveland shot out of the air. Suddenly Golden State was on the offensive with a chance to tie—or take the lead.

Moments like this were exactly why the Warriors had brought Kevin to the team. And this was exactly the type of moment Kevin had hoped would come when he'd signed with Golden State. He hadn't played for the Warriors in 2015–16 when they'd fallen short of winning The Finals. In the offseason that followed, Golden State signed Kevin as a free agent because the team felt it lacked one more player who could come up big in the sport's loneliest of moments—when the pressure of roaring fans and high stakes cause nerves to fray. They felt they needed someone who could close out games, like tonight, and thus would ensure that another LeBron-style comeback never happened again.

Officially Kevin is listed at six foot nine, but he's admitted that in his signature Nikes, he stands seven feet tall. He said he likes being listed as shorter than his true height as a joke, part of his fun, free-spirited personality.

He'd always been the tallest anyway—the tallest in his class in kindergarten, fourth grade, and middle school. He was this skinny kid who kept growing and growing and growing while being raised in Prince George's County, Maryland, just outside of Washington, DC. As much as his height helped him become a talented basketball player, it was his arms that set him apart even in the NBA, where almost everyone is tall.

With his arms stretched out, Kevin's wingspan measured seven foot five end to end, and somehow he was still coordinated. He could shoot and dribble like someone a foot shorter. Yet he could rebound and block shots in a way no six-foot guard could even dream of doing.

So snagging that rebound was the easy part. What to do next was the tougher decision.

There were about fifty-one seconds remaining in the game. Golden State needed a basket. It needed a hero.

Kevin had always felt he was built for these kinds of make-or-break scenarios. His combination of size and skill made him nearly impossible to defend. He felt that when his team needed to score, he was the one capable of doing it, especially in big games.

Yet getting to the ultimate pressure-filled stage, The Finals, had proven difficult for him throughout his career. He'd spent eight years playing for the Oklahoma City Thunder (and one year prior when the team had been based in Seattle and was called the SuperSonics). He'd reached one NBA Finals in 2012, but lost to LeBron, who was playing for Miami then.

Kevin was twenty-two years old at the time and thought he'd return regularly to The Finals.

He didn't. Oklahoma City always fell short. Sometimes it was in the Western Conference Finals. Sometimes it was due to injury. Whatever it was, Kevin couldn't get the NBA championship that he coveted.